Rational
Expectations

RATIONAL
EXPECTATIONS

Macroeconomics
for the 1980s?

Michael Carter
The Australian National University

and

Rodney Maddock
The Australian National University

MACMILLAN

First published 1984 by
Higher and Further Education Division
MACMILLAN PUBLISHERS LTD
London and Basingstoke
Companies and representatives
throughout the world

Printed in Hong Kong

British Library Cataloguing in Publication Data
Carter, Michael
Rational expectations
1. Macroeconomics
I. Title   II. Maddock, Rodney
339   HB 172.5
ISBN 0–333–33143–5
ISBN 0–333–33144–3 Pbk

To Jenny, Chris and Juan

Contents

Preface

Once again, macroeconomics is at the forefront of economic debate. Theory and practice are pursued with a vigour not seen since the Great Depression and the days of Keynes. If there is a single focal point of the modern debate, then it is surely rational expectations. The theory of rational expectations was presented to the economics profession as a rationale for its own impotence. A deceptively simple concept, its implications appeared at first to be radical and profound. With the passage of time, a more secure analysis of the impact of rationality is now emerging. The rational expectations revolution has highlighted some of the shortcomings of the orthodox Keynesian synthesis which guided economic policy through the 1950s and 1960s. But has it provided a better alternative theory to guide policy in the 1980s? Our book seeks to answer this question.

It does not purport to be a comprehensive survey of all that has been written on the subject of rational expectations. That task has been undertaken by others. Nor, certainly, does it claim to be an authoritative and ultimate assessment of an era in economic thought. Our book has much more modest objectives. We have aimed to set out the central ideas of rational expectations in a macroeconomic context in a manner which we hope is accessible to beginning students. We also hope that it will prove of value to those non-professionals with some background in economics who are mystified by the intellectual basis of current macroeconomic policy. Much of the literature on rational expectations is abstruse in the extreme. Our task has been to present the essence of this work in a simple and coherent fashion. Wherever necessary, we have not hesitated to substitute clarity for rigour. We encourage the reader who is curious about the finer points to consult the original journal articles. Indeed, a subsidiary aim of this book is to equip the motivated reader to tackle the journal literature.

There is a strong theme underlying our book – namely, that economic research does not proceed serendipitously like the drunk's random walk. Rather, the direction of economic research responds to the state of the world. Rational expectations came along when it did because of the demonstrated failure of pre-existing theory to explain the dismal economic performance of the period. But economic researchers also tend to act like the drunk who looks for his car key under the light of the lamp-post rather than in the dark where he dropped it. They like to cling to familiar territory, they are reluctant to abandon a line of research even if there is mounting evidence that the key is not to be found there. There is a tendency to focus on problems which are tractable though less relevant. These characteristics of economic research are evident in the story of rational expectations. Indeed, we believe that the development of the theory becomes much clearer if it is viewed from the perspective of an evolving research programme. We have highlighted this methodological perspective and organised our presentation in historical fashion. Methodologists will recognise a strong Lakatosian (Lakatos, 1970) flavour. This makes the development of rational expectations more transparent. In addition to its intrinsic interest, the story of rational expectations is of interest as a case study in the development of economic thought. We hope that the book might be useful supplementary reading for courses in economic methodology or the history of economic thought.

The book traces its heritage to a well-received article published in the *Journal of Economic Literature* (Maddock and Carter, 1982). Readers of that article might wonder what has happened to Bert and Ernie. We can assure you that they are alive and well and have not given up arguing with one another about the world of economics. However, we felt that they had reached their limit in this particular topic. A more conventional presentation was better suited to a book-length exposition. Naturally, the book covers a lot more ground than the article and reflects, we hope, the development of our own understanding in the intervening time. Nevertheless, the article still offers an entertaining introduction to some of the main issues canvassed in this book.

We have one significant apology to make – to our friends who work within the post-Keynesian and radical economics traditions. Such scholars have made a number of powerful and important criticisms of the macroeconomic approach discussed in this book. These include the nature of capital, the complete uncertainty of the future, the role of institutions, of time and of history. Rational expectations theorists have taken little notice of these questions. Thus it has not been necessary for us to dwell on these issues and we have been able to develop our story within the theoretical framework provided by the neoclassical synthesis. By omitting reference to these criticisms which arise outside the rational expectations research programme, we do not mean to imply that they are unimportant or inconsequential. Rather, we judge that they have not played a significant role in the development of the rational expectations programme so far and therefore fall outside the scope of this book.

Every author is only too well aware that he or she cannot write a book alone. Our own debts are many and we can only single out a few for special mention. We have benefited of course from help and encouragement from our colleagues, especially Jeff Borland, Malcolm Gray, Fred Gruen, Ian McLean, Nils Olekalns and Adrian Pagan. Jenny Anderssen, Cherie Cromwell, Eva Klug and Doug Whaite, always willing and competent, provided invaluable research assistance. The fine environment and facilities provided by the Institute of Advanced Studies at the Australian National University have greatly facilitated our work. Finally, we wish to acknowledge the role of our wives, Colleen and Marleny, without whose warm support and understanding little would have been achieved.

We have made a determined effort to write this work in a non-sexist manner. Since established habits are very hard to overcome, even this goal is probably less than perfectly achieved. For this and all shortcomings of this book, we of course assume full responsibility.

Michael Carter
Rodney Maddock

Oil prices: exogenous shock

hits .mcᶜ shift to mc

as it is assumed to ↑P

Introduction 1

Macroeconomic theory has changed profoundly in the last ten years. Where economists once debated whether fiscal policy was more effective than monetary policy as a tool of macroeconomic management, they now argue about whether the macroeconomy can be managed at all. This bout of pessimism seems to have derived from two inter-related phenomena – the persistent high levels of inflation and unemployment in many countries of the world and the advent of a new set of theoretical propositions in economics, loosely termed *rational expectations macrotheory*. Not only do national economies seem to be out of control but a theory has emerged to tell us that there is little we can do about it.

The central feature of this new class of economic theory is its concern with expectations. Economists have long recognised the importance of expectations in explaining the tendency of market economies to fluctuate in their levels of activity. Whenever somebody buys a new car, or any other durable good, he or she is making a decision about the future. Implicit in the decision is some expectation of future prices or future employment prospects. A belief that oil-prices will rise, an expectation of a price rise, will normally be reflected in the purchase of a vehicle with good fuel economy. The decision to finance the purchase by borrowing under a time-payment plan again reflects the belief that one will retain one's job. Equally the decisions of private corporations or government production units to invest in new plant and equipment reflects their expectations. Union wage negotiations reflect the same concerns.

1

Keynes recognised this crucial role played by expectations of the future and pointed to the investment function of businesses as the central cause of the volatile behaviour displayed by capitalist economies. In his argument, business investment depended crucially on the mood of investors. Animal spirits, business confidence, or the mass psychology of groups of investors became a control focus of his analysis.

Rational expectations theorists also recognise the crucial role played by expectations but with a very different perspective. Expectations become explicit predictions about the level or rate of change of some economic variable based on use of the best model and all the information available. Whereas with Keynes' model expectations formation seems to be placed outside economics and within the domain of psychology, the vision of expectations within the new class of models is of a rational economic prediction based upon economic models. All macroeconomists recognise the importance of expectations, and what rational expectations theorists have done differently is to demonstrate to economists a *new* way of dealing with expectations in their models.

On its own ground, rational expectations theory would merit attention from economists since it demonstrates how expectations can be incorporated into the corpus of economic theory in a consistent way. Its importance in macroeconomics has been heighted by the implication that, in a world of rational expectations, government demand management policy is ineffective. Whereas in a Keynesian world the confidence of investors could be boosted by an increase in aggregate demand engineered by government fiscal or monetary policy, in a rational expectations world government *can achieve nothing* of the sort. To a generation of economists who grew up thinking that the problems of the Great Depression could never recur this result came as quite a shock. It assured rational expectations theory a very prominent place in the discussion of macroeconomics in the 1980s.

We will show in later chapters that the ineffectiveness proposition is not an inevitable consequence of the use of a rational expectations model. It does appear from within the particular theoretical framework adopted by many of the early contributions and is the most outstanding result to arise from the rational expectations literature. There are a variety of models, even Keynesian ones, which assume expectations are formed rationally but which allow for an effective demand management policy.

Rational expectations theory is worthy of study for its role in modern macroeconomics. However, we believe that the way in which the theory has developed is also of great interest to the student of economics. Therefore, the main focus of this book will be on *the development of macroeconomic theory* and not upon the implications for society of the theoretical results. We intend to explore the way rational expectations theory evolved, its response to challenges and its search for empirical verification. In addition we will consider the way in which the existing orthodox economic theory responded to the challenges thrown out to it by rational expectations theory and theorists. By this we hope to achieve two goals – to enable our reader to understand the strengths and weaknesses of the theory, and at the same time to learn more about the way macroeconomic research is actually carried out. Before proceeding we will deal with two preliminary matters. Section 1.1 considers the way theories develop following their own internal criteria while Section 1.2 deals with the relation between theory and society.

1.1 Theory Development

As one might expect there are a number of different views about how economic theories develop. Perhaps the simplest adopts an evolutionary perspective wherein new and better theories replace outmoded versions. Usually some crucial experiment is considered to have demonstrated the superiority of the new over the old. Some problem is discovered with a current version of a theory, a modification is made to deal with the anomaly and then it is tested to see whether or not it has adequately resolved the difficulty.

This is a very handy vision of the progress of knowledge. Under it young economists (or scientists) have only to learn the very latest version of the theory and the rules for testing new versions which might be necessary in the future. The most current theory contains the distilled wisdom of all that has gone before; earlier variants have been proved wrong and hence are inferior and unnecessary. The rules for testing theories have to be learnt because they enable economists to distinguish good variants of the theory which might emerge from bad ones.

Unfortunately, though, the actual practice of economics is quite different. There are a number of basic visions of the nature of the economy and they compete with one another to demonstrate the superiority of their approach and their models. This competition between theories is one of the dynamic forces which leads to the development of theory. Broadly speaking, there are two main competing visions in contemporary economics – the activists and the passivists. The activists assume that national economies do not settle down into nice, stable equilibrium positions employing the resources of the society at an optimum level. The label 'activist' arises because they believe that government can and should intervene to stabilise the economy and to ensure that it settles at a level of activity which does not leave unutilised labour and capital. The passivists, on the other hand, think that economies will achieve socially desirable equilibrium positions unaided, and that government action is either irrelevant or positively harmful. We have already suggested that one of the main purposes of this book is to illustrate the struggle between the schools over the idea of rational expectations and the way in which that struggle has led to the development of macroeconomics. To understand macroeconomic theory one has to see the way the competition amongst groups of economists with different visions over an idea such as rationality of expectations leads to a development of both their views.

Although there are other visions of macroeconomics, the activists and the passivists share certain common perceptions. They believe that insight is gained into macroeconomic processes by consideration of competitive situations where individuals make optimising decisions. Discussions of monopoly power, exploitation, and so on, are ruled out. They believe that empirical evidence is important in the assessment of theories. We will see that advocates of each side use a variety of methods in trying to convince economists generally of the validity of their propositions. Appeals are made to intuition, logic and algebra, to one's prejudices and to one's appreciation of elegance or simplicity, but almost invariably there is also an appeal to the data. Fortunately the formalised testing procedures of econometrics are accepted by both the activists and the passivists involved in the debate over rational expectations so that the empirical discussions have been substantial and important. The methods themselves have changed during the decade of the 1970s but both sides have felt it important for rational expectations theorists to demonstrate econometrically the validity of their arguments. This common ground has been important. When 'Keynesians' and monetarists could never agree during the 1960s about the efficacy of fiscal and monetary policy the main problem seems to have been that one group thought that the realism of models was the important test of validity, the other that prediction was the key. In the rational expectations debate the prediction criterion has been generally accepted, although the theory has often been criticised for its lack of realism. This substantial agreement on method enabled a debate to develop in which the two sides communicated and had a real influence over the nature of each other's work. Often economists of different persuasions seem to argue at cross purposes. But, in this literature, this seems not to have been the case.

Two visions of the economy have clashed over rational expectations and they have genuinely communicated. So should we expect a victor to emerge? We think not. Despite sharing similar beliefs about the importance of econometric testing there has been no decisive experiment. Visions in economics are complex and theories based on them are difficult to test. One cannot decide between one and the other merely on the basis of a single test. In fact one has to make so many auxiliary assumptions to set up an econometric test of a theory that it seems that there will always be grounds for one side to find fault with the other's experiment. One has usually to simplify the theory to obtain an obviously testable proposition, to assume a variety of other factors unimportant, to obtain data that approximates the theoretical concepts and to find the appropriate econometric tests. At each of these stages critics will inevitably be able to find fault. For these reasons there is no evidence of a critical experiment resolving any major controversy in economics.

The inability of economists to resolve their disputes decisively is one of the things which complicates economic thought. Virtually no explanation of the causes of inflation has ever been disproved. This has meant that during the inflation of the 1970s the analyses of the cause, and hence of possible solutions, we extremely diverse. Unions were blamed, governments were blamed, foreigners were blamed and so on. Economic propositions are embedded in social phenomena. To test the economics we must either control the social aspects or make assumptions about them. Since generally we cannot control the social environment our tests are always open to the criticism that the particular assumptions made were invalid.

Because we cannot easily clear away the ground surrounding economic theories, we cannot easily rank the standing of competing theories. To understand how 'good' one group of theories is compared with another we are forced to analyse the development of the theory, to see whether or not it is progressing. One of the objectives of this book to show how the struggle to obtain decisive support for a given set of propositions has a creative influence on the development of theory.

We shall see that in the case of rational expectations theory the process of trying to provide convincing tests of their propositions did lead theorists to *develop* their theory. They did not convince people of the merit of their views on the basis of their tests – most of the tests they performed in support of their theories turned out to be inconclusive. Rather than convince outsiders of the value of the theory, the tests provided by Sargent and later Barro (see Chapter 5) led those writers and others to realise some of the inadequacies of the models they were proposing and *to improve them*. In this view the role of testing in economics is not to convince people but to enhance one's own research programme. This is clearly an overstatement. Models are often estimated to provide a guide to the effects of a policy change, and the *cumulation* of successful tests often sways outsiders to pay greater credence to a theoretical programme. However, in this book, we hope to demonstrate that the most important role of testing in the rational expectations programme has been to stimulate the development of the theory. By concentrating our attention on the way in which the rational expectations programme has developed over time we expect to demonstrate to the reader the importance in understanding an economic 'theory' that is gained by consideration of how it got to its present state, to show the role of failed experiments and the role played by theorists working in different research programmes.

1.2   Theory and Society

In the previous section we discussed the way theories arising out of different visions interact with one another and with the data available and in the process are changed and modified. However in social sciences there are other forces at work which influence theory development. Social science theories are about people and they influence the way people actually behave, especially the way in which governments behave. Broadly one might say that people look to them for guidance about how to behave or, having decided how to behave, use them to justify their behaviour. In the words of Keynes:

> **The ideas of economists and political philosophers, both when they are right and when they are wrong, are more powerful than is commonly understood. Indeed, the world is ruled by little else.**
>
> (Keynes, 1936, p.383)

Macroeconomic theory in particular is closely aligned with the behaviour of governments. Keynes was specifically concerned to persuade policy-makers to change their behaviour during the Great Depression. Subsequently, variants of his theory were developed to relate policy 'instruments' controlled by the authorities to the current state of the economy, specifically to the levels of income and unemployment. It is often useful to think of macroeconomics as comprising the theories of macroeconomic policy and policy-making. The image of governments fine-tuning the economy, manipulating the controls to steer the economy towards desirable outcomes guided by macroeconomic theory, became the dominant view of the 1960s.

Governments of the period were guided in their behaviour by theory, and by their faith that the theory was appropriate to achieve the preferred social objectives. A period of successful management along these lines led governments to believe that they could steer the economy along the preferred paths and they built this belief into their political rhetoric. Whereas the pre-Keynesian view had seen the capitalist economy as something prone to booms and slumps with government and society responding to its fluctuations, the attitude which came to dominate after the Second World War was that government was able and indeed bound to *control* capitalist economies. So ingrained was this perception that economists and political scientists came to speak of political business cycles in which governments deliberately induced small cycles in the economy in order to enhance their electoral prospects. While capitalist economies had been seen as innately prone to fluctuations, governments came to insist that they controlled the macroeconomic outcomes. They were guided in this by their faith in the theory.

This intricate involvement of theory with political practice produced problems for the theory with the advent of stagflation in the early 1970s. Table 1.1 shows the sharp decline in growth rates, increases in inflation and in unemployment which characterise this period. None of the countries in the table was able to find a macroeconomic policy which governments were willing to implement and which would eliminate unemployment and inflation. From a position where governments had been perceived to be able to direct the macroeconomy – to be 'super-potent' – the dramatic turnaround shown in the table had both political and theoretical consequences. As to the former, governments tended to be voted out of office. Further, the view of the government having access to super-potent policies for manipulation of the economy had been based on (activist) macroeconomic theory. Not only was the political myth of government control over the economy broken but it also broke the faith of economists in the decisive power of fiscal and monetary policy.

As might be expected the theoretical challenge was led by passivists, but their arguments took a new twist. While they had always opposed the activist orthodoxy of the 1960s they now insisted that the phenomenon of stagflation had been *caused* by activist policies. Led by the rational expectations theorists they charged that governments had no power to change levels of employment by demand-side policies and that if such policies were attempted inflation would result. The focus of their analysis was still on the role of government, but on its inevitable impotence rather than on its ability to do good.

Thus, as we suggested in the previous section, the rise of rational expectations theories can be seen as a new round in the battle between activists and passivists. Its *timing* can be explained by the sudden inability of older activist policies to eliminate stagflation. This failure itself threw doubt on the dominant activist theories and the pressure on the older theoretical position was accentuated by the political difficulties faced by the government which had convinced most voters that they could handle the economy. The social role of the theory contributed to its sudden fall from grace.

TABLE 1.1
Growth Rate of Real GDP at Market Prices (Percentage Changes)

	1965	1970	1975	1980
United States	6.0	−0.1	−0.1	−0.2
Germany	5.6	6.0	−1.8	1.8
United Kingdom	2.3	2.2	−0.8	−1.8
Canada	6.8	2.6	1.1	0.1
Australia	5.7	6.2	2.4	2.9

Unemployment Rates (Per cent of Total Labour Force)

	1965	1970	1975	1980
United States	4.4	4.8	8.3	7.0
Germany	0.3	0.8	3.7	3.1
United Kingdom	2.3	3.1	3.9	7.4
Canada	3.6	5.6	6.9	7.5
Australia	1.5	1.6	4.8	6.0

Changes in Consumer Prices (Percentage Changes from Previous Year)

	1965	1970	1975	1980
United States	1.7	5.9	9.1	13.5
Germany	3.4	3.4	6.0	5.5
United Kingdom	4.8	6.4	24.2	18.0
Canada	2.4	3.3	10.8	10.1
Australia	4.0	3.9	15.1	10.2

Source: *OECD Economic Outlook*, no. 29, July 1981, pp. 132, 142, 140 respectively.

As conservative governments tended to replace activist ones, the need appeared for a new 'conservative' theory to guide and/or justify conservative policies. Rational expectations theories, and other theories which focussed on the supply rather than the demand side of economics, fulfilled this role. Such theories suggested that there was little the government could do about unemployment and that attempts to eliminate it by demand management policies would create inflation. These propositions provided much of the ideological justification for conservativism. Without potent demand-side tools governments were 'forced' to rely on providing incentives to capitalists and investors to expand supply and, as the benefits of this expansion 'trickled down' to the rest of the economy, the benefits would be shared.

Thus we see the *social* role of the theory having two levels of influence on the practice of economics. First the timing of the appearance of the new theories can be explained by the need to resolve a new phenomenon, stagflation. Secondly, the collapse of activist governments and their replacement by conservative governments required the development of a new economic theoretical justification of the policies they chose to adopt. Thus we explain the appearance and success of this new variant of passivist theory. Other new theories were stimulated by the collapse of the older orthodoxy – political business cycle theory for example. However these did not fit the justificatory role. Periods of theoretical crises in all sciences tend to spawn a variety of new theories. Which of the emerging variants tends to be successful depends on a variety of grounds such as theoretical consistency or empirical support, but in social science theory, the social and ideological role played by the theory can also be important.

1.3   Conclusion

Rational expectations theory emerged as the bright new theoretical star of the 1970s. Older demand management theories had been tarnished by the appearance of stagflation. This book takes the reader step by step through the major developmental steps of the new theory. There are two preliminary steps – Chapter 2 explains the gradual evolution of the concepts of expectations from Keynes to rational expectations while Chapter 3 outlines the basic macroeconomic arguments necessary to understand the subsequent developments. The strong form of the rational expectations model – the demonstration that government policies of macroeconomic demand management are impotent – is developed in Chapter 4. From this high point of passivist rhetoric we retreat a little to consider some of the challenges to this assertion made by economists of different persuasions. There are challenges to the validity of the basic model of the economy employed, challenges to the assumption that people do have rational expectations, and questions of whether they can. This chapter is followed by one where we consider the ways in which the advocates of the rational expectations model developed their theory in the light of both these theoretical challenges and their own failures to produce any convincing empirical evidence in support of their propositions. Because economists argue with one another on the basis of logic, evidence, style and so on, it can be difficult to pin down exactly why rational expectations theorists modified their models. We have chosen to show the developments in the context of testing failures (reinforced where necessary by other arguments) because of the importance which macroeconomists seem to place on testing.

The final chapter draws together the various developments. We ask two basic questions – what have rational expectations theorists learnt about their models and methods from the challenges thrown at them and what changes to activist-type theories seem necessary in the light of the arguments and evidence for rational expecta- tions? The important point is that neither side has won the war but that each has learnt from the battles. We believe that the continuing failure of the rational expectations theorists to extract any convincing empirical evidence is gradually weakening their position but that their challenges have caused important reformu- laions of activist thought.

One of the main objectives of this book is to show how economic theories develop through a process of interaction with one another and by the use of a variety of tools. Rational expectations theories are one of the important competing research programmes of the 1980s and our readers should better under- stand what they are and what they mean. They should also understand the ways in which the clash with rational expectations theorists has influenced other macroeconomic theory. By under- standing this process of dynamic change within competing theories we expect our readers to be better equipped to understand future developments.

Expectations in Economics

The major theme of this book is the theory of rational expectations and its role in modern macroeconomics. In this chapter, we depart somewhat from that theme and introduce rational expectations in a *microeconomic* context, where the impact of expectations is more readily apparent. In this way, we hope to highlight the role of expectations and give some practice in utilising expectations-based models. We briefly consider the role of expectations in economics, and outline the historical antecedents of rational expectations. Then we introduce the notion of rational expectations into the familiar context of a simple cobweb model and show how this modification radically alters the results obtained.

2.1 What are Expectations?

Expectations (in economics) are essentially forecasts of the future values of economic variables which are relevant to current decisions. For example, firms have to forecast the future prices for their products (and those of their potential competitors) in order to decide how much to produce in the current period, and whether or not to invest in new equipment. Similarly, farmers have to forecast future prices for various crops in order to determine which crops are most profitable to plant. Union negotiators have to predict the future rate of inflation in their wage bargaining.

Households have to make implicit or explicit forecasts of future prices in deciding whether to purchase a house, a car or a washing machine. In particular, they have to forecast the price of money, namely the rate of interest.

Expectations, then, are the decision maker's forecasts or predictions regarding the uncertain economic variables which are relevant to his or her decision. Two important points should be noted:

● Expectations are essentially subjective – the personal judgements of a particular individual. They do not have an independent existence apart from the person or decision-maker who holds them. Although we will later talk of the expected price in a given market, we are really referring to some aggregate of the expectations of all the individual agents in the market.

● An expectation regarding a particular economic variable need not be confined to a single predicted value. It is better regarded as a complete probability distribution over future values of the variable. However, in our discussion, this will often be summarised by the mean. Indeed, it can be shown that this involves no loss of generality provided that the models are linear.

Since virtually all economic decisions involve taking actions now in return for uncertain rewards in the future, expectations of the future are crucial in decision-making.

Although the importance of expectations in eocnomics has long been recognised, one of the first economists to give expectations a paramount role in his analysis was John Maynard Keynes. Generally regarded as the foremost economist of this century, Keynes revolutionised the study of macroeconomics in his book, *The General Theory of Employment, Interest and Money* published in 1936. This work will figure prominently in later chapters.

While expectations play a role in Keynes' earlier writings, they take centre stage in his *General Theory*. His analyses of the level of employment, the demand for money, the level of investment and the trade cycle all depend crucially on expectations. For example, in discussing the determination of the level of employment, Keynes wrote:

Thus the behaviour of each individual firm in deciding its daily output will be determined by its short-term expectations – expectations as to the

cost of output on the various possible scales and expectations as to the sale-proceeds of this output ... It is upon these various expectations that the amount of employment which the firms offer will depend. The *actually realised* results of the production and sale of output will only be relevant to employment in so far as they. cause a modification of subsequent expectations.

(Keynes, 1936, p. 47)

In fact, it is perhaps reasonable to assert that the Keynesian revolution in economics *was* the elevation of uncertainty and expectations to a prominent place in economic analysis (Davidson, 1972).

Despite the leading role given to expectations in his work, Keynes did not really address the question of how expectations are formed. Moreover, since his treatment was theoretical and discursive rather than analytical and empirical, his notion of expectations was a long way from an operational concept. [1] A great deal of research work in macroeconomics, particularly in recent times, can be seen as an attempt to convert the Keynesian expectations-based theory into an operational theory with testable hypotheses. Ironically, as we shall see, much of this research effort has downgraded the crucial role of uncertainty in expectations and has produced results at odds with those developed by Keynes.

Before considering these macroeconomic issues let us look at the ways in which expectations have been formalised in economics. We will use a simple cobweb model as a vehicle for this discussion.

2.2 The Cobweb Model

The cobweb model of a market is familiar to nearly all students of economics. While it is usually presented as an example of dynamics and market stability, it is also the first formalisation of expectations in an economic model which most students of economics encounter. This makes it a useful starting point for our exposition.

The essence of the cobweb model is some delay between the formation of production plans and their realisation. It is therefore

---

[1] In economics, as in other sciences, a concept is said to be operational when it is expressed in terms of quantities which are observable and can be measured. Expectations *per se* are not directly observable.

often applied to agricultural markets, where farmers decide in one season how much land to plant in a crop which will be harvested in a subsequent season. By the time of the harvest, the quantity of the crop available (the supply) is determined and the price which prevails is that which clears the market. But how does the farmer decide how much to plant? To make this decision he has to form some expectation of the price that will prevail when the crop is harvested and marketed. The simple hypothesis which drives the cobweb model is that the farmer bases his expectation of future prices on the price ruling at the time of planting. Since all farmers follow the same rule, the model predicts that a year of glut will be followed by a year of shortage followed by another year of glut and so on in the familiar cobweb pattern which gives the model its name. Under certain conditions, the oscillations will converge to equilibrium; under other conditions, not.

We can formalise the above discussion as follows. Demand in period t depends upon the price in period t, which we represent with the following linear demand function:

$$q^d_t = \alpha - \beta p_t \qquad \text{(demand)} \qquad (2.1)$$

Where q^d_t is the quantity demanded in period t, p_t is the market price in period t, and α, β are constants. The quantity supplied in period t depends upon the price which farmers *expected would prevail at marketing time* when they made their planting decisions. That is, it depends on the price expected for period t, which we shall denote by p^*_t. Therefore, the supply is given by:

$$q^s_t = \gamma + \delta p^*_t \qquad \text{(supply)} \qquad (2.2)$$

where q^s_t is the quantity supplied in period t, and γ and δ are constants. In any period, the actual price that prevails will be such that the quantity demanded is equal to the quantity supplied, so that the market 'clears'. Therefore, we must add a third equation to our model which represents the condition for market equilibrium:

$$q^d_t = q^s_t = q_t \qquad \text{(market equilibrium)} \qquad (2.3)$$

Utilising equation (2.3) to equate the right-hand sides of equations (2.1) and (2.2), we can solve for p_t in terms of p^*_t, obtaining:

$$p_t = (\alpha - \gamma)/\beta - (\delta/\beta)p^*_t \qquad\qquad (2.4)$$

Equation (2.4) gives us an expression for the actual price in each period as a function of the expected price in each period. Since we cannot directly observe the p^*_t, our model is not operational – it contains unknown variables. To make it operational we need to specify the determination of p^*_t, preferably in terms of variables already in the model.[1]

The simple hypothesis which closes the cobweb model is that each farmer forms his expectations in the preceding season, and bases his expectation of next season's price on the current market price. That is, the cobweb model has an additional behavioural equation:

$$p^*_t = p_{t-1} \qquad \text{(Expectations)}$$

Substituting this equation in equation (2.4), we can derive another expression for p_t. We call this equation the *reduced form equation* for prices since it relates the price level to known constants α, β, γ, δ and the known past variable p_{t-1}:

$$p_t = (\alpha - \gamma)/\beta - (\delta/\beta)p_{t-1} \qquad\qquad (2.5)$$

To illustrate the properties of equation (2.5), let us consider a simple numerical example. Assume that the parameters of the demand and supply functions have the following numerical values: $\alpha = 416$, $\beta = 2$, $\gamma = -64$, $\delta = 1$. We also need to assume an initial starting position for the market – let us assume that the price in period 0 is 192. $p_0 = 192$. This implies that $p^*_1 = 192$. Table 2.1 traces out the behaviour of the model for the succeeding six periods (the reader is invited to verify the calculations).

Examination of Table 2.1 shows that in this case the model converges gradually to the equilibrium values of $p = 160$ and $q = 96$. However, in the process, both prices and quantities deviate considerably from the equilibrium. Moreover, the oscillations follow a regular pattern, in which periods of low supply and high price are followed by periods of high supply and low price. This

---

[1] This process of expressing variables in terms of other variables in order to make a model operational is often called 'closing the model'.

Table 2.1
The Cobweb Model: A Simple Numerical Example

Period	P^*	P	q
1	192	144	128
2	144	168	80
3	168	156	104
4	156	162	92
5	162	159	98
6	159	161	95

gives rise to the familiar cobweb pattern illustrated in Figure 2.1.

Not surprisingly, the cobweb model does not attract much empirical support (Coase and Fowler, 1935) since it assumes that farmers conduct their business in a most naive manner.

● First, their behaviour ignores the impact of similar actions of all the other farmers. For example, consider period 2, in which supplies are short and consequently prices are high. This induces each farmer to plant a much larger crop for next year in the expectation that the high price will be maintained, but since all the other farmers will react in the same way, total supplies will be much greater in the next year. Surely the farmers will appreciate that their combined actions will lead to a sharp increase in supply which will depress prices.

● Second, even if they are not sufficiently smart to consider the impact of their joint actions, one might reasonably expect the farmers to learn from their experience and to benefit from that knowledge. The cobweb market follows a very regular pattern, which reveals itself readily – namely, oversupply, undersupply, oversupply, undersupply. The assumptions of the cobweb model do not allow for any learning at all on the part of the farmers.

FIGURE 2.1
The Cobweb Model

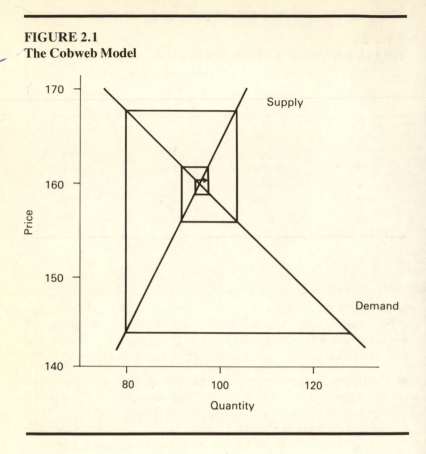

As a model of expectations, the cobweb model is thus unsatisfactory. However it does illustrate the importance of expectations and highlights the advantages of alternative models of expectations.

2.3   Extrapolative Expectations

In an attempt to eliminate the extreme naivety of cobweb models, Metzler (1941) introduced the idea of *extrapolative expectations*. He reasoned that future expectations should be based not only on

Table 2.2
Extrapolative Expectations: A Simple Numerical Example

(a) $\epsilon = 0.5$

Period	P^*	P	q
1	192	144	128
2	120	180	56
3	198	141	134
4	122	180	58
5	198	141	134
6	122	180	58

(b) $\epsilon = -0.5$

Period	P^*	P	q
1	192	144	128
2	168	156	104
3	150	165	86
4	161	160	97
4	161	160	97
5	162	159	98
6	160	160	95

the past level of an economic variable, but also on its direction of change. Thus, if p_{t-1} represents the price level in period t_{-1}, and p_{t-2} the price level in period t_{-2}, the extrapolative prediction for period t is defined as:

$$p^*_t = p_{t-1} + \epsilon(p_{t-1} - p_{t-2}) \tag{2.6}$$

where ϵ is called the *coefficient of expectation*.

The extrapolative expectation in any period is equal to the price level in the previous period plus (or minus) some proportion of the change between the previous two periods. If ϵ is greater than zero, then past trends are expected to be continued, whereas if ϵ is less than zero, past trends are expected to be reversed. For $\epsilon = 0$, extrapolative expectations are identical to the naive cobweb model.

The effect of imposing extrapolative expectations on the cobweb model is illustrated in Table 2.2 for two different values of the coefficient of expectation, ϵ. The other parameter values are the same as those used in Table 2.1.

In Table 2.2(a) we see an example in which the model shows no obvious tendency to converge to the equilibrium values. Rather, the prices and quantities oscillate markedly above and below the equilibrium. However, in Table 2.2(b), we use a negative coefficient of expectation and there the model converges slightly faster to equilibrium than in the classical cobweb case (cf. Table 2.1). As these two examples demonstrate, the extrapolative mechanism allows for more variety in the behaviour of the model.[1]

The behaviour of the model with extrapolative expectations is governed by the value of the coefficient of expectation, ϵ, the best choice of which depends upon the underlying economic structure of the model. In this case, negative values of ϵ are clearly more appropriate. High prices stimulate production which increases supply in the subsequent season and lowers prices again. In other words, price trends tend to be reversed rather than maintained from year to year. This is a simple demonstration of the notion that the appropriate expectations mechanism depends upon the structure of the model.

2.4   Adaptive Expectations

A similar mechanism of expectations formation, usually attributed to Cagan (1956), has been used more frequently in economics. According to this definition, agents revise their expectations each period according to the degree of error in their previous expectations – hence the name *adaptive expectations*. Using the same symbols as above, the adaptive expectation (made in period $t-1$) of the price level in period t is defined as:

$$p^*_t = p^*_{t-1} + \eta(p_{t-1} - p^*_{t-1}) \tag{2.7}$$

---

[1]In mathematical terms, the simple cobweb model is a linear first-order difference equation; when associated with an extrapolative expectations mechanism, it becomes a second-order difference equation model. Second-order equations have a much richer dynamic behaviour.

where 'η' is called the coefficient of adaptation. It determines the speed at which expectations adjust to past errors. For a technical reason which will be explained below, 'η' lies between zero and one. Thus, with adaptive expectations, the expected value in the next period is equal to the expectation for the current period plus or minus a proportion of the error in the expectation for the current period. If 'η' is equal to 1, then equation (2.7) reduces to:

$$p^*_t = p_{t-1}$$

The relationship between extrapolative and adaptive expectations can be seen more clearly if we transform the preceding equation. First, by grouping similar terms, we can rewrite the equation as:

$$p^*_t = \eta p_{t-1} + (1-\eta)\, p^*_{t-1} \qquad (2.8)$$

The second variable on the right-hand side, p^*_{t-1} is the expectation (formed in period $t-2$) of the price level in period $t-1$. It will be related to the previous period's expectation according to the formula:

$$p^*_{t-1} = \eta p_{t-2} + (1-\eta)p^*_{t-2}$$

which is simply equation (2.8) with t replaced by $t-1$ and $t-1$ replaced by $t-2$. Substituting this equation into equation (2.8), we obtain an expression for p_t^* in terms of p_{t-1}, p_{t-2}, and p_{t-2}^*:

$$p_t^* = \eta p_{t-1} + \eta(1-\eta)p_{t-2} + (1-\eta)^2 p^*_{t-2} \qquad (2.9)$$

Proceeding in a similar manner, we can express p^*_{t-2} in terms of variables relating to period $t-3$, that is

$$p_{t-2}^* = \eta p_{t-3} + (1-\eta)p^*_{t-3}$$

Substituting this equation in equation (2.9), we obtain yet another expression for p^*_t:

$$p^*_t = \eta p_{t-1} + \eta(1-\eta)p_{t-2} + \eta(1-\eta)^2 p_{t-3} + (1-\eta)^3\, p^*_{t-3}$$

$$(2.10)$$

Clearly, this process of expressing one period's expectation in terms of values relating to the preceding period and substituting in equation (2.8) can be carried out indefinitely. At each step, we obtain an expression in which p^*_t is equal to the weighted sum of a series of past prices plus the expectation at an earlier period. But note that as we proceed with the substitution, the weight attached to the expectation declines. This is the technical reason for requiring 'η' to be less than 1. For example if $\eta = 0.5$, equation (2.10) is:

$$p^*_t = 0.5p_{t-1} + 0.25p_{t-2} + 0.125p_{t-3} + 0.125p^*_{t-3}$$

and the weight attached to the expectation term p^*_{t-3} after only three substitutions is 0.125. It can be shown (the type of argument is probably familiar from calculus) that as the substitution is carried out a large number of times, it tends to a limiting value in which the expectation term is zero. Thus, we arrive at a formula in which p^*_t is expressed in terms of a weighted average of all preceding actual prices:

$$p^*_t = \eta p_{t-1} + \eta(1-\eta)p_{t-2} + \eta(1-\eta)^2 p_{t-3} + \eta(1-\eta)^3 p_{t-4} +$$

$$\eta(1-\eta)^4 p_{t-5} + \eta(1-\eta)^5 p_{t-6} + \dots$$

In future we will represent such an infinite sum with the following notation:

$$p^*_t = \eta \sum_{k=1}^{\infty} (1-\eta)^{k-1} p_{t-k} \tag{2.11}$$

This is an example of a construct which is very common in economics. It is called a *distributed lag* because the weight is distributed over a number of lagged (past) values. In equation (2.11) the weights have a very special form – they form a geometric series (remember $0<\eta<1$). A generalised distributed lag representation for p^*_t is given by:

$$p^*_t = \sum_{k=1}^{\infty} w_{k-1} p_{t-k} \tag{2.12}$$

where the w_{k-1} are arbitrary weights. (w_{k-1}) must be such that this sum converges.

Both extrapolative and adaptive expectations are just special cases of this general form. Adaptive expectations is the case in which the weights are given by:

$$w_k = \eta(1-\eta)^k$$

that is

$$w_1 = \eta(1-\eta)^0 = \eta$$
$$w_2 = \eta(1-\eta)^1$$
$$w_3 = \eta(1-\eta)^2$$

as can be seen by comparing equations (2.11) and (2.12). Extrapolative expectations is the case in which the weights are given by:

$$w_1 = 1 + \epsilon$$
$$w_2 = -\epsilon$$
$$w_k = 0, k > 2$$

This can be seen clearly if we rewrite equation (2.6) as

$$p^* = (1+\epsilon)p_{t-1} - \epsilon p_{t-2}$$

This means that an extrapolative expectation is based only on the information contained in the actual values for the preceding two periods. An adaptive expectation, on the other hand, is based on the entire past history of the series.

Until the recent introduction of the idea of rational expectations, adaptive expectations was the most common formalisation of expectations used in economics. Its popularity was due to its conceptual simplicity and the ease with which it could be implemented empirically. Statistical estimates for the coefficient of expectation 'η' can easily be obtained. Moreover, adaptive behaviour in the face of an uncertain environment appears intuitively very plausible and appealing. Adaptive expectations models appeared to work well in an environment in which change was gradual – a characteristic of the 1950s and 1960s. Yet there are obvious problems associated with the use of an adaptive expectations mechanism:

● The intuitively plausible adaptive mechanism is formally equivalent to a distributed lag with geometrically declining weights. Yet there is no real justification for such weights. As can be seen from the general form, there is an infinite variety of weighting systems for implementing a distributed lag expectations mechanism, and geometrically declining weights is just one special case. [1]The virtue of geometric weights is of course that it makes it easy to estimate, but that provides no support for any claim that it validly represents actual behaviour.

● Adaptive expectations incorporate only past values of the variable being forecast. It seems likely that considering past values of variables other than the one being forecast may enable the decision-maker to make better forecasts. This intuition can be shown to be true except under fairly restrictive conditions. Moreover, there may be contemporaneous information available to the forecaster which is highly relevant to the variable being forecast. For example, knowledge of which party has just won a general election may be used to improve a forecast of inflation which is otherwise based solely on past price data.

● Mechanical application of an adaptive expectations formula, therefore, does not necessarily make best use of all the information available. For this reason it is suspect as a description of economic behaviour.

Let us consider a simple hypothetical example which illustrates this point and serves to introduce the idea of rational expectations to be considered in the next section. Assume that the economy behaves in such a way that the level of prices is always a simple

---

[1]Consider, for example, the case in which the series p is strongly seasonal and the periods are quarters. Then the immediately preceding quarterly observation p_{t-1} assumes the most weight in forming the prediction. However, the lower-weighted quarterly observation p_{t-4}, which relates to the corresponding period in the previous year, may be of more relevance for the prediction. This could be allowed for in the general distributed lag model, but not in the more specialised adaptive model.

function of the money supply:[1]

$$p_t = 2M_t \tag{2.13}$$

Assume that the government is able to determine the money supply, M_t, and that it follows the rule:

$$M_t = 20 + 3(t-1964)$$

which simply states that the money supply is increased by three units each year (that is, $M_t = 20$ in 1964, 23 in 1965, and so on). Assume further that this rule is known to, and believed by, all agents in the economy. Finally assume that expectations are formed adaptively with coefficient of expectation equal to 0.5, i.e.

$$p^*_t = p^*_{t-1} + 0.5(p_{t-1}-p^*_{t-1})$$

and that for 1964 expectations are correct, i.e.

$$p_{1964} = p^*_{1964} = 40$$

Then, the behaviour of the economy over the succeeding four years is depicted in Table 2.3:

Table 2.3
Adaptive Expectations $\eta = 0.5$

Year	M_t	p_t	p^*_t	Error
1964	20	40	0	
1965	23	46	40	6
1966	26	52	43	9
1967	29	58	48	10
1968	32	64	53	11

[1]What we really mean here is that this equation is the reduced form of the 'true' model of the economy. It is an equilibrium relationship and we are assuming that the equilibrium is achieved rapidly.

Under these particular circumstances, the adaptive expectations mechanism performs poorly. Rather than converging to zero, the expectation errors increase from year to year. Before going on to consider a better expectations mechanism, we would like to make three more points.

1. Note that in this model the higher the value of coefficient 'η', the better the forecasts. Recalling that 'η' is restricted to lie between 0 and 1, the optimum value of 'η' is 1 for this example. However, as we noted before, adaptive expectations reduce to the cobweb model when 'η' is equal to 1. Therefore, the cobweb assumption is superior to more general adaptive expectations in this particular case.
2. Recall equation (2.11) which represents the adaptive expectation of p at time t as the weighted sum of all past values of the p with geometric weights. One property of this equation is that the expected value of p can never be greater than the maximum previous value of p.[1] This is a general property of adaptive expectations.
3. Note that our assessment would be different if we were forming expectations about the change in the price level rather than the absolute level of prices. In our example, the price level increases by six units every year and an adaptive expectations mechanism would rapidly converge on this value. This is a further illustration of the intimate link between expectations and the structure of the economic model. The interested reader might like to do the arithmetic for this example.

In summary, then, adaptive expectations are effective when the variable being forecast is reasonably stable, but adaptive expectations are of little use in forecasting trends. This we suggest is why adaptive expectations were popular in the 1950s and 1960s when inflation rates were low and relatively stable. When inflation accelerated, adaptive forecasts were left further and further behind.

We have demonstrated the inappropriateness of adaptive expectations in this very simple example. But a much superior expectations-generating (forecasting) method immediately sug-

---

[1] The weights form a geometric series which sums to 1. If you would like some practice in manipulating these series, you might try proving the assertion made in this paragraph.

gests itself. Since the government follows a fixed rule which is known and since the economy follows the reduced form in equation (2.13), economic agents can use this information to form perfect forecasts of future prices. The optimal forecasting rule is given by:

$$p^*_t = 2M_t^*$$
$$= 40 + 6(t-1964)$$

We suggest that the reader work out the behaviour of the economy using this forecasting rule and verify that expectations errors are indeed zero.

Consider now a slightly different case in which the government does not follow any fixed rule in determining the money supply, but for any period *it is publicly announced* in the preceding period. We continue to assume that the behaviour of the economy is described by equation (2.13). Then, economic agents can again make perfect forecasts of future prices by utilising the publicly announced money supply figures, according to the formula:

$$p^*_t = 2M_t^* \tag{2.14}$$

Of course, in the real world, the government cannot determine exactly the money supply. But they do provide money supply targets in their budget announcements, and provided the behaviour of the economy is reasonably predictable, it is hard to believe that this information will not be used by economic decision-makers.[1]

We would like to pause and reflect for a moment on the preceding two paragraphs. In the first case, the price level is determined by a simple linear function of the money supply and every agent in the economy is assumed to know this relationship. The money supply in turn is determined by a fixed rule which is also known to all agents. Equipped with this information, agents are able to make perfect predictions of future price levels. Surely they will do so? In the second case, the government does not follow a fixed rule. Instead, it announces each period the money supply in the following period. Again, this is sufficient to make

---

[1] Of course, the qualifying clause in the previous sentence is all important and the focus of much of the debate.

perfect predictions about the next periods price level. Surely agents will use this information in forming their predictions?

This is the essence of the idea of rational expectations. Over time, economic agents accumulate a wealth of information concerning the relationships governing economic variables and the behaviour of other agents, including in particular the government. This information can be used in forming expectations about future values of economic variables. It is to this idea that we now turn.

2.5   Rational Expectations

So far we have discussed three different expectations mechanisms – the naive cobweb assumption, extrapolative expectations and adaptive expectations. All three suffer from a common failing: they are essentially arbitrary, rather than based on any underlying theory of economic behaviour. Since the formation of expectations is an integral aspect of economic behaviour, cannot the tools of economics be applied to this aspect? Why not develop an economic analysis of the formation of expectations in the same way as economic principles are used to analyse other market behaviour?

Questions such as these led to the publication in 1961 of a now classic paper in which John Muth advanced the 'rational expectations' hypothesis. In his own words:

> I would like to suggest that expectations, since they are informed predictions of future events, are essentially the same as the predictions of the relevant economic theory ... The hypothesis asserts three things: (i) information is scarce, and the economic system generally does not waste it; (ii) The way expectations are formed *depends specifically on the structure* of the relevant system describing the economy; (iii) A 'public prediction' ... will have no substantial effect on the operation of the economic system (unless it is based on inside information).
>
> (Muth, 1961, p. 316; emphasis added)

The fundamental premise on which most economic analysis is based is that economic agents 'do the best they can with what they have'. Muth reasoned that information should be considered as just another of the resources available to be allocated to maximum advantage. Utility-maximising individuals should use all the information available to them in forming their expectations. Part of the information which is relevant to the behaviour of any economic system is the structure which underlies that system. Therefore, Muth concluded, rational economic agents would use their knowledge of the structure of the economic system in forming their expectations.

Before we go on to develop a rational expectations model, we need a slight digression. One of the objectives of this book is to equip the reader to read research articles in the area. Much of this work relies on concepts and terminology from the theory of probability, especially stochastic processes. One of our difficulties has been to estimate the statistical background of our readers. To make the book as self-contained as possible, we have provided a short appendix to this chapter which presents the necessary background in superficial, but we hope intelligible, form. We will draw freely on these ideas in what follows, and we urge the reader to review the appendix before proceeding.

The meaning of the rational expectations hypothesis can best be shown by a simple example, which is adapted from Muth 1961. The model is a version of the cobweb model discussed in the previous chapter, with the addition of a stochastic term (u_t) in the supply function.

$$q^d_t = \alpha - \beta p_t \tag{2.15}$$

$$q^s_t = \gamma + \delta p^*_t + u_t \tag{2.16}$$

$$q^d_t = q^s_t = q_t \tag{2.17}$$

where q^d_t = the quantity demanded in period t, and q^s_t is the quantity supplied in period t. u_t is a random variable, representing for example variations in crop yields due to the weather. In other words, supply in any period depends on two factors: the amount planted (which in turn depends upon the expected price) and the yield, which is represented by the random variable u_t.

By simple manipulation of the model, we can derive the following expression for prices (the reader is urged to carry out the derivation):

$$p_t = (\alpha - \gamma)/\beta - (\delta/\beta)p^*_t - (1/\beta)u_t \tag{2.18}$$

The actual price in any period depends upon the expected price and upon the yield. Except for the random term, this equation is identical to equation (2.4) above. As discussed there, to complete ('close') the model, we need to provide an expression for the expected price, p^*_t. Here we come to a crucial point. The innovation introduced by Muth was to consider the expected price as endogenous to the model, and generated by the model itself. The agents in the market are assumed to know the structure of the model as represented in equations (2.15) – (2.17) and to use this information in order to form their expectations. We can put this formally by stating as an assumption that the expected price in any period is equal to the mathematical expectation conditional on the information available in the previous period. This information includes of course the precise structure of the model (that is, equations (2.15) – (2.17)).

In other words, we introduce into the system an additional behavioural equation which embodies the hypothesis of rational expectations, namely:

$$p^*_t = E_{t-1}(p_t) \tag{2.19}$$

where E_{t-1} [ ] is the mathematical expectation conditional on the information available in period $t - 1$.[1] Therefore, the full model with the addition of the rational expectations hypothesis is:

$$q^d_t = \alpha - \beta p_t \tag{2.20}$$

$$q^s_t = \gamma + \delta p^*_t + u_t \tag{2.21}$$

$$q^d_t = q^s_t = q_t \tag{2.22}$$

$$p^*_t = E_{t-1}[p_t] \tag{2.23}$$

---

[1] The mathematical expectation conditional on the information available in period $t - 1$ is often written $E[Xt:I_{t-1}]$, where I_{t-1} denotes the information available in period $t-1$. We use the notation E_{t-1} since it makes the longer expressions less complicated.

Applying equation (2.23) to equation (2.18), we obtain:

$$p^*_t = E_{t-1}(p_t)$$
$$= E_{t-1} \left[(\delta - \gamma)/\beta \right] - E_{t-1}[\delta/\beta)p^*_t] - E_{t-1}[(1/\beta)u_t]$$
$$= (\alpha - \gamma)/\beta - (\gamma/\beta)p^*_t - (1/\beta)E_{t-1}[u_t]$$

Rearranging this equation to solve for p^*_t, we obtain:

$$p^*_t = (\alpha - \gamma)/(\beta + \delta) - 1/(\beta + \delta) \times E_{t-1}[u_t]$$

Let us define the new variable $\bar{p}$ equal to the constant on the right hand side, i.e.:

$$\bar{p} = (\alpha - \gamma)/(\beta + \delta)$$

Then we have:

$$p^*_t = \bar{p} - 1/(\beta + \delta) \times E_{t-1}[u_t] \qquad (2.24)$$

It can be shown (the reader is invited to confirm this) that $\bar{p}$ is equal to the equilibrium price in the market, that is the price such that:

$$p_t = p_{t-1} = p_{t-2}$$

when

$$u_t = u_{t-1} = u_{t-2} = 0$$

Therefore, the expected price in any period is equal to the equilibrium price plus a multiple of the mathematical expectation of the random variation in supply, where the expectation is conditional on the information available in period $t-1$. This in turn depends on the probability distribution of the random variable u_t.

Recalling now the material discussed in the appendix, the sequence of random variables (u_{t-1}) comprises a stochastic process. We can consider two different hypotheses concerning the distribution of the terms of the stochastic process, depending on whether or not successive terms of the stochastic process are independent. Let us consider these two separate possibilities for the probability distribution of u_t.

Case (i) {u_t} are uncorrelated

In this case, the random shocks u_t are analogous to the tosses of a 'true' die. Each random variable is completely unpredictable and in each period

$$E_{t-1} [u_t] = 0$$

The past history of the series (u_t) contains no information which can be used for predicting future values. Substituting the preceding equation in equation (2.24), we derive the following expression for p^*_t:

$$p^*_t = K$$

The rational expectation of the price in each period is the equilibrium price. Remember that participants in the market are assumed to know the structure of the market as represented by equations (2.20) – (2.22). Therefore, they can compute the equilibrium price level. In any period, this equilibrium price level is the rational expectation of the actual price. Compare this with the cobweb model, in which the expected price is equal to the price in the previous period. This induces cycles in the actual price which will be absent in the rational expectations model. The actual price will equal the equilibrium price plus a random but independent disturbance.

Case (ii) {u_t} is serially correlated

The case in which the process (u_t) is serially correlated is more interesting. Moreover, we would expect the (u_t) in our model to be serially correlated, since it represents the impact of the weather on crop yields. As discussed in the appendix, if the supply disturbances (u_t) are seriously correlated, then past history of the series contains information relevant to predicting its future values. This information is available to the decision-maker at time $t-1$. Therefore, according to the rational expectations hypothesis, this information will be used in forming expectations. Recall from the appendix that, provided it is linear, the process (u_t) can be represented as a weighted sum of independent random variables with zero mean, as follows:

$$u_t = \sum_{k=0}^{\infty} w_k \epsilon_{t-k}$$

and therefore that the expected value of u_t is equal to:

$$E[u_t] = \sum_{k=1}^{\infty} w_k \epsilon_{t-k} \tag{2.25}$$

since

$$E[\epsilon_t] = 0$$

and

$$E[\epsilon_{t-k}] = \epsilon_{t-k} \qquad k>0$$

where all expectations are made at time $t-1$.
Substituting equation (2.25) into equation (2.24), we obtain:

$$p^*_t = \bar{p} - 1/(\beta+\delta) \times \sum_{k=1}^{\infty} w_k \epsilon_{t-k} \tag{2.26}$$

and substituting this in turn into equation (2.18), we obtain an expression in which p_t is expressed as a sum of independent random variables:

$$p_t = \bar{p} + \sum_{k=0}^{\infty} v_k \epsilon_{t-k} \tag{2.27}$$

where the weights v_k are functions of the parameters α, β, γ and δ of the demand and supply functions. Provided the weights v_k satisfy a certain condition, equation (2.27) can be equivalently expressed as:

$$p_t = \bar{p} + \sum_{k=1}^{\infty} v'_k (p_{t-k} - \bar{p}) + v'_0 \epsilon_t \tag{2.28}$$

Taking the expected value of equation (2.28), we can derive an expression for p^*_t in terms of past values of p_t:

$$p^*_t = \bar{p} + \sum_{k=1}^{\infty} v'_k(p_{t-k} - \bar{p}) \qquad (2.29)$$

where again the weights v'_k are functions of the parameters of the demand and supply functions.

Equation (2.28) looks superficially similar to the adaptive expectations formula of the previous section. The important difference is that, in this case, the weights in the distributed lag are not governed by an *ad hoc* geometrically declining formula, but are determined by the coefficients of the demand and supply functions of the original model. That is, the expectations-generating mechanism depends directly on the structure of the model. It is in this sense that the expectations are endogenous in a rational expectations model.

In some ways, Muth's choice of example was unfortunate, for it is a special case. It is not generally true that a rational expectation of a single variable can be expressed as a distributed lag of the past history of that variable alone. Muth's example is special in that a random element enters into only one of the behavioural equations, in this case the supply function. Let us therefore consider the implications of introducing random variation into both the demand and supply functions. The new model comprises:

$$q^d_t = \alpha - \beta p_t + w_t$$

$$q^s_t = \gamma + \delta p^*_t + u_t$$

$$q^d_t = q^s_t = q_t$$

$$p^*_t = E_{t-1}[p_t]$$

In this case, the rational expectation of p^*_t cannot be expressed as a distributed lag on past prices alone. It is necessary to utilise the information contained in the past history of the quantity series as well (Nelson, 1975).

We can form an expression for p^*_t in which it is expressed as a distributed lag of past prices. Further, there will be some choice of coefficients which gives superior predictions to any other choice – this is known as the *optimal extrapolative predictor*. But expectations formed only on the basis of past price data will have greater variance than the rational expectation, which takes into account the information contained in past quantities as well as past prices. Muth's example is a special case in which the optimal extrapolative predictor and the rational expectation are equivalent.

By means of these examples, we have shown that adaptive expectations and rational expectations are related. Rational expectations makes two major advances over adaptive expectations.

- Rational expectations provides a basis for calculating the weights to be used in the distributed lag. In fact, the weights depend explicitly on the structure of the economic model.
- Except in very special circumstances, a rational expectation will depend on more than simply the past history of the variable to be predicted.

2.6   Conclusion

Although the importance of expectations in economics has long been recognised, attempts to formalise the role of expectations are relatively recent. Early formalisations, such as extrapolative and adaptive expectations, relied on arbitrary assumptions regarding the expectation formation mechanism which had little if any economic content, but the formation of expectations and the processing of information are activities to which the tools and concepts of economics can be applied.

Very broadly, then, rational expectations can be viewed as the application to the process of expectation-formation of the same analysis as is applied to the models in which expectations are embedded. In this way, we would like to suggest that *rational expectations theory a 'natural' development of the progress of economic science*. Previously, expectations had been treated on an *ad hoc* basis. The introduction of rational expectations enabled expectations to be treated consistently with other economic variables. Therefore, it is intuitively satisfying to the economist. It is founded on the very plausible assumptions that information is scarce and not wasted and that the way in which expectations are formed depends upon the structure of the model.

Some reservations must be expressed immediately. First, conviction is not empirical support. However plausible rational expectations might seem from the economist's armchair, the hypothesis is of little value in explaining behaviour if the world works in a different manner. The information requirements for truly rational expectations are quite heroic, and there is considerable doubt as to whether these requirements are met. This will be discussed later. Second, although assuming that expectations are formed rationally results in a considerable conceptual simplification of expectations-based models, it makes these models more difficult to manipulate and estimate. This second proviso will not be discussed directly in our work (see, for example, Wallis, 1980).

Appendix: Some Topics from Probability Theory

In many places in this book, it is necessary for us to use certain concepts and terminology from probability theory. To make the book as self-contained as possible, we have here gathered together some necessary background. Our treatment is necessarily superficial but we hope that it is intelligible. For lucid and well-motivated treatment of this material, we recommend Gottman (1981).

Random variables and expectations

Suppose that a rich uncle offers to toss a die and pay you one pound for each dot in the result. How much would you expect to receive? Of course, after the toss, the result is known exactly. But before the event, what would be your best guess? The possible outcomes are 1, 2, 3, 4, 5 or 6, which may be interpreted either as the number of dots or the number of pounds transferred. Each of these outcomes has a probability of 1/6.

The number of dots resulting from a toss of a die, or equivalently the number of pounds which your uncle will give you, is an example of a *random variable*. Roughly speaking, a random variable is a variable which can take on one of a range of values (real numbers) depending upon the outcome of an as yet undetermined event. The likelihood of any given value being generated is governed by the probability distribution associated with the random variable.[1] The probability distribution governing the toss of a die is simply that there are six possible outcomes [1, 2, 3, 4, 5, 6], each of which is equally likely. Therefore the probability of any individual outcome, for example a 2, is one chance in six.

Now to return to our first question, how much might you as an individual nephew expect to receive from your uncle's offer? The amount of money you would expect to receive *prior to the toss* is called the *expected value* of the random variable. The possible outcomes are 1, 2, 3, 4, 5 or 6 dollars, and each of these has a probability of 1/6. The expected value is equal to the sum of the outcomes weighted by their respective probabilities, i.e.

$$\text{Expected value} = 1 \times \tfrac{1}{6} + 2 \times \tfrac{1}{6} + 3 \times \tfrac{1}{6} + 4 \times \tfrac{1}{6} + 5 \times \tfrac{1}{6} + 6 \times \tfrac{1}{6}$$

$$= (1 + 2 + 3 + 4 + 5 + 6) \times \tfrac{1}{6}$$

$$= 3.5$$

More generally, if x is a random variable which can take on the values $(x_1, x_2, x_3, \dots, x_n)$, each with an associated probability p_1, $p_2, p_3, \dots p_n$, the expected value of X, denoted $E[X]$, is defined as:

$$E[X] = \sum_{i=1}^{n} x_i p_i$$

$E[X]$ can conveniently be thought of as a weighted average value, where the weights are the probabilities of the respective outcomes. Note that the expected value may not be one of the possible outcomes. This is illustrated in the die example, where the expected value is 3.5, which is not a possible outcome of the toss of a die. The expected value of a random variable is also known as the *mean*. It is the average expected in a large number of trials.

One way to view the expected value of a random variable is that it is a *summary measure* combining both the range of possible outcomes and the probability distribution. Obviously, it is impossible to collapse all the information concerning a random variable into a single number such as the expected value. Therefore, the

---

[1] More precisely, the set of possible values plus the associated probability distribution together constitute a random variable.

expected value only captures a portion of the total information regarding a random variable. There are many other summary measures which capture other aspects of the character of the random variable. Prominent among other useful summary measures of a random variable is the *variance*. The variance is a measure of how far, on average, individual observations tend to deviate from the expected value. We will desist from giving a formal definition of the variance here, referring the interested reader to any text on probability. Instead, let us consider an example. Adult males do not vary much in height. Except for a few extreme examples, the range of observed heights is small and most adult males are close to average height. Contrast this with weight, where the range is very much greater. We say that height has a low variance, whereas weight exhibits a high variance.

Some properties of expected values are used in the text. First, the expected value of a constant is of course the constant. That is, if X is a (degenerate) random variable which takes only a single value γ, then the probability of γ is one, and

$$E[X] = \gamma \times 1 = \gamma$$

Second, the expected value of the sum of two random variables is equal to the sum of their expected values. That is, if X and Y are random variables:

$$E[X + Y] = E[X] + E[Y]$$

This extends in an obvious way to the sum of an indefinite number of random variables. But note that, except in a very special case, the expected value of the product of two random variables is not equal to the product of their expected values.

We have now used the term 'expectation' in two different senses in this book. The concept that we have just been discussing is strictly termed *mathematical expectation*. It is a mathematical operator which assigns to any random variable a particular summary measure, its mean. It must be clearly distinguished from the concept of expectation as prediction or anticipation held by economic agents in formulating their plans, which is the main topic of this book. The former is a strictly mathematical property of probability distributions; the latter is a behavioural concept in economics. A decision-maker may have expectations regarding many different aspects of a random variable, of which its mathematical expectation (expected value) may be only one. However, in much of the literature, it is implicitly assumed that the expectation is confined to the expected value.

When no other information is available, the mathematical expectation is the best possible predictor of the average expected outcome. This was the case in the die-tossing example. However, in economics, other information is frequently available which can be used to improve the prediction. In essence, the information modifies the probability distribution of the outcomes. It can be shown that the best prediction when further information is available is the so-called *conditional expectation*, which is the mathematical expectation calculated with the modified probability distribution.

Stochastic processes

Often we are not merely interested in a single random variable, but in a sequence of related random variables. For example, in macroeconomics we are concerned with the passage of an economic system through time. If the system is subject to random shocks, these will occur repeatedly rather than only once. The random component is then properly treated as a sequence of related random variables.

A sequence of random variables is known as a *stochastic process*. For example, a single toss of the die is a random variable. If the die is tossed repeatedly, the series of outcomes is a stochastic process. Just to make the ideas concrete, imagine that the die is tossed five times. Each toss gives rise to a different random variable – we can label these $x_1, x_2, \ldots, x_5$. A particular outcome of the 5 tosses will be a sequence of numbers representing the result of each toss. This is known as a realisation of the process. The sequence 4, 3, 2, 2, 6 is one possible realisation, where 3 is the outcome of the second toss. We will use the notation (x_t) to represent a stochastic process, where x_t represents the random variable which constitutes the process.

Repeatedly tossing a 'fair' die is not a very interesting example of a stochastic process. This is because each toss of the die is independent of all the other tosses. In general, the random variables constituting a stochastic process are not independent; their dependence not only makes their behaviour more interesting, but it can be exploited for analysis. That is, if the random variables of a stochastic process are dependent, this knowledge can be used to derive information about unobserved variables from those that are observed. We will see this idea recur throughout the book.

To illustrate the idea of dependence, consider the example of the stochastic cobweb model developed in the text. Equation (2.16) extends the earlier supply function (equation (2.2)) by adding a random variable, u_t. This is motivated as representing for example, the effect of the weather on crop yield and hence supply. If we are interested in the market over more than one period, the collection of the variable u_t representing the weather in each period is a stochastic process. Not only is the weather in each period a random variable, it is not independent of the weather in other periods. The stochastic process (u_t) in our stochastic cobweb model is a dependent stochastic process.

Instead of dealing with dependence and independence, statisticians prefer to use the related property of *correlation*. We will not give a formal definition of correlation here; again the interested reader will find this in any text on probability. For our purposes it suffices to say that two random variables are correlated if they are related in such a way that they tend to move together or in opposite directions.[1] Higher-than-average values of one random variable are generally observed at the same time as higher-than-average values of the other. Barometric pressure is a good example of a correlated stochastic process. Since atmospheric pressure changes only gradually, days on which the pressure is higher than average tend to be followed by similar days. Similarly, low pressures tend to persist for more than one day. Any other random variable representing the weather is likely to exhibit correlation. In fact, any stochastic process of which the random variables exhibit cyclical behaviour will be correlated. Most economic variables are correlated. On the other hand, the random

---

[1] We remind our statistically-inclined readers that independent random variables exhibit zero correlation, but that the absence of correlation does not imply independence.

variables representing successive tosses of a 'true' die are uncorrelated – each toss is independent of all the other tosses.

For an uncorrelated stochastic process, the outcomes of individual random variables convey no information about other outcomes. For example, the fact that the second toss of the die yielded a '5' does not help us predict the third toss. On the other hand, for a correlated stochastic process, knowledge of the value of one element conveys some information about the values of other elements. For example, one would be unlikely to predict rain tomorrow purely on the basis that it has not rained for a while. Rather, the fact that it rains today may increase our perceived likelihood that it will rain tomorrow. Similarly, the past history of the price level in an economy provides information relevant to the prediction of future values.

We now show precisely the sense in which past values of a stochastic process provide information relevant to the prediction of future values. Assume that the stochastic process (u_t) is *stationary* – that is, its probability distribution does not change through time. Then, any element of the stochastic process u_t can be written as a sum of uncorrelated random variables v_{t-k}, each of which has zero mean, that is:

$$u_t = \sum_{k=0}^{\infty} v_{t-k}$$

where

$$E[v_t] = 0$$

The random variables v_{t-k} are called the *innovations* of the process. In other words, for every linear stationary stochastic process, there exists an associated *uncorrelated* stochastic process of innovations which generates it, in the sense that each term in the original process can be written as the sum of all the preceding innovations. [1]We can derive a similar expression for the expected

---

[1] This rather surprising theorem (Wold, 1938) is worth remembering since it clarifies much of the empirical work on rational expectations. Strictly, any stationary process can be decomposed into two uncorrelated components, one of which is purely deterministic and the other purely non-deterministic. A purely non-deterministic process can be predicted from its own past values without error. The above representation as a linear sum of innovation applies to the purely non-deterministic component (Priestley, 1981, p. 756).

value of u_t. Assuming that all except the current innovation are known at time t, the expected value of u_t conditional on the information available at time $t-1$ is:

$$E_{t-1} [u_t] = E[u_t : v_{t-1}, v_{t-2}, v_{t-3}, \ldots]$$

$$= E_{t-1} [v_t] + \sum_{k=1}^{\infty} v_{t-k}$$

$$= \sum_{k=1}^{\infty} v_{t-k}$$

since

$$E_{t-1} [v_t] = 0$$

$E[X:I]$ denotes the expectation of the random variable X conditional on the information set I. Therefore, the expected value of u_t in any period t is equal to the sum of all the past values of v_t. Provided that the expression above meets certain conditions, this expected value can be equivalently expressed in terms of past values of u_t rather than past values of v_t:

$$u^*_t = \sum_{k=1}^{\infty} w_k u_{t-k}$$

That is, the expected value of u_t in any period is equal to a weighted sum of all the past values of u. Since the past values are assumed to be known when the expectation is formed, the expected value can be derived merely from a knowledge of the series.

To recapitulate, providing a stochastic process is stationary, the past history of the process itself can be used to predict its future values. We note however that a linear combination of the past observations may not necessarily be the best possible prediction if additional information (for example the history of a statistically related stochastic process) is available. This distinction arises in the text when we compare adaptive and rational expectations.

Demand Policies to Reduce Unemployment 3

The central problem of macroeconomic policy is generally seen to be the management of the level of aggregate activity in the economy so as to achieve certain desired goals such as full employment and the absence of inflation. In this chapter we consider some of the economic theory required for an understanding of the macroeconomomic policy problem.

What then is a policy? Consider the problem of driving a car into a garage. The driver has a well-defined objective or *target*, namely to manoeuvre the car into a certain location without colliding with any obstacles. He or she has available certain *instruments*: the steering wheel, the accelerator and the brakes. The problem is to choose through time a suitable combination of the instruments so as to achieve the target. The most suitable choice of instruments depends upon the behaviour of the car and its current location. This example illustrates all the essential ingredients of a policy problem: one or more targets, one or more instruments, an initial position and a set of rules governing the motion of the system over time. In the example of the car, the set of rules is Newtonian physics. The solution of the problem, that is a particular sequence of speed and direction, constitutes a *policy* for this problem.

In the case of macroeconomic policy, the targets are states of the economy such as low unemployment and inflation and the instruments are monetary and fiscal policy. The rules governing the motion of the economic system over time depend upon the structure of the economy and the behaviour of all its participants.

Since these rules are extremely complex and (currently) unknown, they must be represented by a suitable model of the economy. In this chapter we consider in turn each of the elements of the macroeconomic policy problem. First, we briefly consider the instruments of economic policy. Then, we consider the set of rules governing the motion of the system – the appropriate model of the economy. This issue is crucial. As we shall see, the debate about the effectiveness of policy when expectations are formed rationally is really a debate about the most suitable model for representing an economic system. We consider the model of the economy in two stages: first we discuss the concepts of aggregate demand and supply; then we consider the phenomenon of inflation and the role of expectations. Finally, we consider the targets of macroeconomic policy and the concept of a *policy rule*.

3.1 The Tools of Macroeconomic Policy

Monetary and fiscal policy then are the instruments of macroeconomic policy. The principal tool of *monetary policy* is control of the total supply of money in the economy. There are many different definitions of exactly what constitutes the supply of money. Basically, money consists of the total amount of cash in the hands of the private sector together with the total of all short-term bank deposits. The supply of such money can be manipulated by *open market operations* – purchases and sales of government bonds by the central bank. Additional tools of monetary policy include the *reserve ratio* (the proportion of their deposits which banks must deposit with the central bank) and the *discount rate* (the rate at which member banks can borrow from the central bank).

Fiscal policy involves the alteration of government expenditure or revenue. Changes in government expenditure require an increase or decrease in purchases of goods and services by the government. Construction of new roads, expansion of government departments and increase in farm subsidies all increase government expenditure. Revenue is altered by changes in tax rates, coverage and thresholds. For example, an increase in the rate of personal income tax will increase the tax revenue; so too will the introduction of a new sales tax. Government transfers such as pensions and unemployment benefits are not part of government expenditure in this sense, being transfers of purchasing power between different sections of the private sector. Typically changes in benefits levels and coverage are regarded as components of fiscal policy only to the extent that the total of taxes minus transfers is altered. It is implicitly assumed in this approximation that the spending propensity of the recipients is identical to that of the taxpayers who finance the benefits. This is an approximation which must be treated with caution.

Within the economics profession there has been a long debate over whether fiscal or monetary policy is the most effective instrument for achieving macroeconomic targets. Much of the debate between the 'monetarists' and 'Keynesians' was over this issue. That debate now seems rather sterile, with a consensus that both monetary and fiscal policy can be effective in appropriate circumstances. The most notable differences between the two as instruments for the achievement of government policy objectives depend on (i) the size of the effect on demand per unit of stimulus, (ii) the speed of the effect, and (iii) the certainty of the effect. Furthermore, fiscal and monetary policy are not independent instruments. Government expenditure must be financed either by taxes or by borrowing, and this financing requirement inevitably has implications for the money supply.

3.2 Aggregate Demand and Supply

The concepts of aggregate demand and aggregate supply play the same central role in macroeconomics that the concepts of demand and supply play in microeconomic analysis. *Aggregate demand* is the total demand for goods and services in the economy. It comprises consumer demand, investment, government spending and exports (less imports). The aggregate demand schedule, depicted in Figure 3.1, shows the relationship between the aggregate demand (denoted by Y) and the price level (P). Like the demand curve for a single product, the aggregate demand curve is downward-sloping.

We assume that the reader is familiar with the *IS–LM* model for determining macroeconomic equilibrium. Recall that the *IS* curve depicts all combinations of output Y and the interest rate r which

FIGURE 3.1
Aggregate Demand

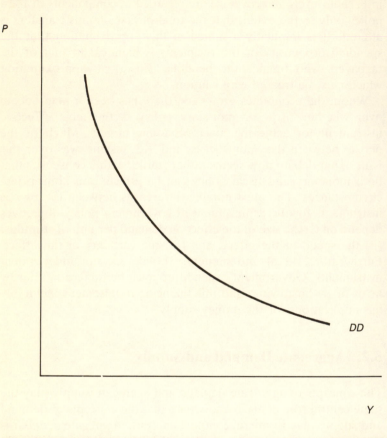

are consistent with equilibrium in the goods market. Similarly, the *LM* curve depicts the equilibrium in the money market. The intersection of the two curves is the point of simultaneous equilibrium in the two aggregate markets. The aggregate demand schedule can be derived within the *IS–LM* framework by considering the impact on the equilibrium of changes in the general level of prices. As the price level rises, the real value of the money supply

FIGURE 3.2
The Derivation of the Aggregate Demand Curve

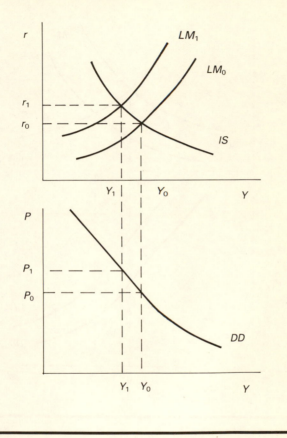

is decreased. This is reflected in a shift upwards in the *LM* curve, leading to a decrease in the equilibrium real income. This is illustrated in Figure 3.2. Suppose the system is initially in equilibrium at output Y_0 and price level P_0. Now assume that the price level is suddenly increased from P_0 to P_1. Assuming no change in the nominal value of the money supply, the real value of the money supply is reduced. This is depicted by the upward move-

FIGURE 3.3
The Effect of Money Supply on Aggregate Demand

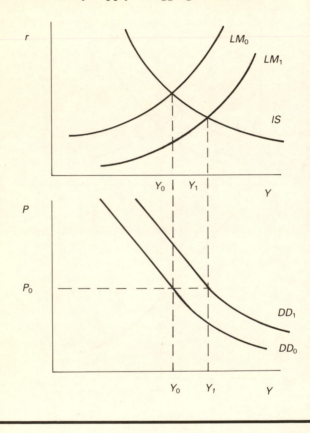

ment of the *LM* curve from LM_0 to LM_1. [1]Output is reduced until equilibrium is restored at level Y_1. The new equilibrium (Y_1 and P_1) lies on the aggregate demand curve. Therefore, the aggregate demand schedule is traced out by movements of the *LM* curve along a given *IS* curve as the real value of the nominal money supply varies with changes in the price level. Higher prices are

[1] We would also expect a downward movement in the *IS* curve, because the price rise will diminish the real value of financial assets, leaving consumers feeling less wealthy. For our purposes, it is satisfactory to ignore this real balance effect.

consistent with lower output, hence the aggregate demand curve is downward sloping.

The *IS–LM* framework can also be used to illustrate the effect of monetary and fiscal policy on aggregate demand. What is the effect, for example, of an increase in the money supply on the aggregate demand curve? Refer to Figure 3.3. An increase in the nominal money supply is depicted by the movement of the *LM* curve from LM_0 to LM_1. This raises the real value of the money supply at any given price level, and consequently the level of aggregate demand consistent with equilibrium at that price level. For a given price level P, equilibrium output increases from Y_0 to Y_1. This corresponds to a rightward shift in the aggregate demand curve from DD_0 to DD_1. Therefore, an increase in the money supply effectively moves the aggregate demand curve to the right. Similarly, an expansionary fiscal policy will also shift the demand curve to the right, although in this case the stimulus works via a movement in the *IS* rather than the *LM* curve.

The aggregate demand curve then depends upon a given mix of monetary and fiscal policy. Expansionary policies move the curve to the right, and contractionary policies to the left. Through appropriate management of the tools of monetary and fiscal policy, the government can manipulate the level of aggregate demand in the economy. But the aggregate demand curve shows that there are an infinite number of possible combinations of aggregate demand and the price level which are consistent with equilibrium in the goods and money markets. To determine which combination of price and demand prevails for given aggregate demand schedule (for a given policy mix), we must consider the aggregate supply curve.

The supply curve of a single firm or industry represents the output that the firm is willing to produce at various prices. Similarly, the *aggregate supply* schedule represents the total amount of goods and services supplied at various price levels (see Figure 3.4). The supply of goods and services in the economy is the output produced by the *employed* productive resources in the economy. These include the services of capital, labour, land, technology and so on. Since time is required to change the stock of capital or to develop new technology, it is common to assume that the supply of capital and other non-labour inputs is fixed in the short run. Then we can consider that the level of output supplied

FIGURE 3.4
The Aggregate Supply Schedule

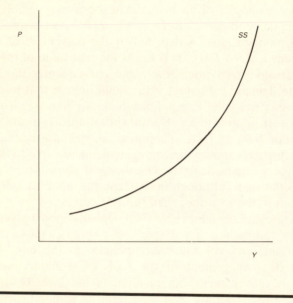

(produced) is directly related to the level of employment. [1]This relationship is depicted in Figure 3.5.

Figure 3.6 combines the aggregate demand and supply curves. With aggregate demand curve DD_0 and aggregate supply curve SS_0, equilibrium is determined at E_0 with output Y_0 and price level P_0. If the government then stimulates aggregate demand through monetary or fiscal policy and moves the aggregate demand curve to DD_1, the new demand curve intersects the aggregate supply curved at E_1. Output will increase to Y_1 (with a corresponding increase in employment), while the price level will increase to P_1.

---

[1] Clearly this relationship is not exact, even if the quantity of labour and capital employed is fixed. Total product might be increased by moving workers from low productivity to high productivity positions without changing overall employment. Moreover, the quantity of capital utilised varies with the state of demand. However, it is a reasonable approximation for our purposes.

FIGURE 3.5
The Relationship Between Output and Employment

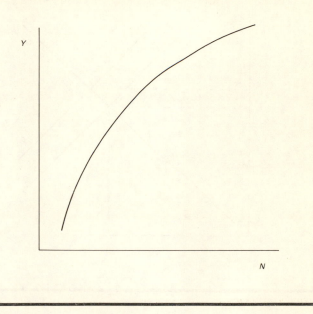

In this way, government policy can alter the level of employment by manipulating aggregate demand.

To summarise then, the government has at its disposal certain policy instruments such as the money supply and tax rates. With these instruments, it can shift the *IS* and *LM* curves. This in turn results in movement in the aggregate demand curve which alters the equilibrium level of output, employment and prices in the economy. Therefore, through its command of the tools of monetary and fiscal policy, the government can to some extent determine the level of employment in the economy.

3.3   The Slope of the Aggregate Supply Curve

We saw in the previous section how an increase in aggregate demand can raise both the level of output and the price level. The

FIGURE 3.6
Aggregate Demand and Supply

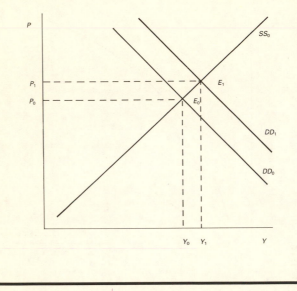

division of the impact between price and output effects depends upon the slope of the aggregate supply curve. Figure 3.7 illustrates two cases. In Figure 3.7(a) the supply curve has a gentle slope. An increase in aggregate demand results in a large increase in output and employment and only a small increase in the price level. Conversely, in Figure 3.7(b) the supply curve is steep. Most of the impact of an increase in aggregate demand is felt in the price level. In the extreme case in which the aggregate supply curve is vertical, changes in aggregate demand can have no impact at all on the level of output or employment. Therefore, the slope of the aggregate supply curve is crucial to the effectiveness of aggregate demand policy. The slope of the aggregate supply curve is determined in the labour market, to which we now turn.

It is customary in macroeconomics to discuss *the* labour market, when in fact it is clear that any real economy encompasses a variety of interconnected labour markets, differing in skills and location. For example, there is a market for physcians in London

FIGURE 3.7
The Relevance of the Slope of the Aggregate Supply Curve

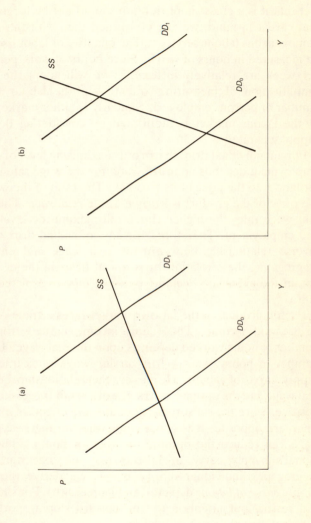

which differs substantially from the market for riggers on the North Sea oilfields. It is obviously a convenient fiction to assume that all these various labour markets can be aggregated together to form a single market for homogeneous labour services. But the fact that it is a gross simplification should not be forgotten. With that caveat in mind, we are concerned then with the market for homogeneous labour services. The quantity of labour services can be measured in hours of work. Since hours of work per employee per week are relatively inflexible, we will adopt the additional simplification of measuring quantity in the labour market by number of persons employed. Similarly to other markets, analysis of the labour market is facilitated by considering demand and supply separately.

For an individual firm, the profit-maximising level of output and employment depends upon the ratio for the wage rate it must pay for labour to the price of its product. The ratio of the wage rate to the price of the product is known as the *real wage*. The lower the real wage rate, the higher the profit-maximising level of output and employment. Therefore, for any individual firm, there is an inverse relationship between the real wage and employment. Aggregating these relationships for all firms in the economy, we obtain the aggregate *demand curve of labour* depicted in Figure 3.8(a).[1]

Each individual in the labour market faces a trade-off between leisure and income. The (real) income earned from a given number of hours worked depends upon the real wage. The optimal number of hours of work for varying wage rates traces out the supply curve of labour. However, the relationship between the real wage and the optimal hours of work is not (necessarily) strictly positive. Since the substitution and income effects of a higher real wage are opposite, it is conceivable that an increase in the real wage can reduce the optimal number of hours. Thus, an individual's supply curve of labour may be 'backward-bending'. Aggregating individual supply curves we derive the aggregate *supply curve of labour* depicted in Figure 3.8(b). For simplicity, we will restrict our attention to the upward sloping portion of the aggregate supply curve of labour.

[1] For a more detailed exposition of the derivation of the demand and supply curves for labour, see for example Branson (1979, pp. 96–107).

FIGURE 3.8
The Demand and Supply of Labour

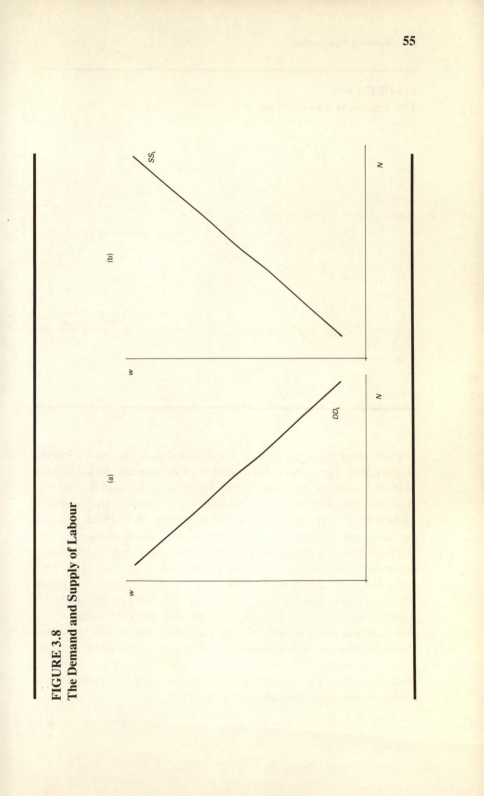

(a)

(b)

FIGURE 3.9
The Aggregate Labour Market

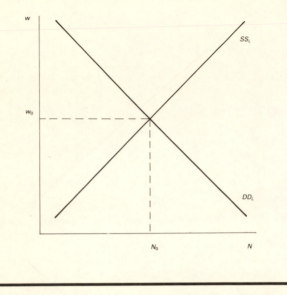

Combining the aggregate demand and supply curves for labour (Figure 3.9) shows the determination of equilbrium in the labour market – namely employment of N_0 at a real wage rate of w_0. Assuming further a direct relationship between the level of employment and the level of output, then the actual level of output is determined by equilibrium in the labour market.

The derivation of the aggregate supply curve can be shown by combining Figures 3.4, 3.5 and 3.9 in such a manner that their common axes are shared. This is done in Figure 3.10 which consists of four quadrants labelled I, II, III and IV. Quadrant III depicts the labour market (Figure 3.9) with the real wage (w) on one axis and employment (N) on the other. Quadrant IV reproduces Figure 3.5 which shows the relationship between employment and output. Quadrant I shows the relationship between output and the aggregate price level, which is the aggregate supply curve. Quadrant II will also be used later.

FIGURE 3.10
The Derivation of Aggregate Supply

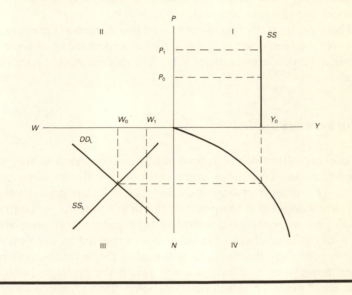

The aggregate supply curve *SS* is derived as follows. Suppose initially that equilibrium is established at P_0 and Y_0. Suppose further that the price level is increased to P_1. Initially this reduces the real wage, increasing the demand for labour while reducing the supply. This disequilibrium in the labour market cannot persist. *Assuming that nominal wages are flexible*, the nominal wage rate will be bid up to counter the excess demand for labour. Equilibrium will be restored when the real wage rate returns to its previous level of w_0, with no change in employment. This implies that output does not respond to a change in prices and therefore that the aggregate supply curve is vertical.

This leaves the macroeconomist in somewhat of quandary. Assuming that prices (including the nominal wage rate) are flexible and that labour demand and supply are determined in a manner consistent with utility and profit maximisation, he concludes that the aggregate supply curve must be vertical. Output must be stable and unaffected by aggregate demand policy. The only impact of a boost in aggregate demand must be a corresponding boost in the price level. Yet experience tells him that aggregate output is far from stable and that it is apparently responsive to changes in aggregate demand.

There are basically two ways around this dilemma. One solution involves the temporary non-fulfilment of expectations; the second solution suspends price flexibility. We discuss each of these in turn.

Workers are fooled

In our exposition of the labour market above we assumed that employers and employees were concerned with the same price level. This is an over-simplification. The relevant price level for the firm's decision is the price of the firm's output. By contrast, employees are concerned with the expected general price level. Any divergence between the price level expected by the firm and that expected by the workers will enable employment to depart from its previous equilibrium level. This is the principle behind a number of models in which demand policy has a temporary effect.

One simple version of this device was proposed by Friedman [1968]. Suppose there is an increase in aggregate demand after a period of stable prices. The expansion puts upward pressure on prices and wages. But since 'selling prices of products typically respond to an unanticipated rise in nominal demand faster than prices of factors of production' (Friedman, 1968, p.10) real wages actually decline. That is, although nominal wages are dragged upwards by the expansion, prices rise faster, so that real wages in fact are lowered. However, Friedman argues, the decline in real wages is *actually perceived* by workers as an increase, since they evaluate the wage offer in terms of the *previous* (lower) price level. Employers perceive a decline in the real wage, prompting them to increase their demand for labour; *simultaneously* employees perceive an improvement in the real wage, persuading them to increase their supply of labour. 'Indeed, [it is] the simultaneous fall *ex post* in real wages to employers and rise *ex ante* in real wages to employees ... [that enables] employment to increase' (Friedman, 1968, p.10).

FIGURE 3.11

Aggregate Supply with Temporary Misperceptions

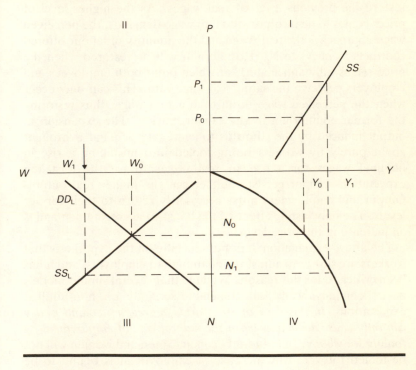

This is illustrated in Figure 3.11. The increase in aggregate demand pushes up prices and wages. But since wage increases lag behind price increases there is a temporary fall in the real wage, say from w_0 to w_1. The change is actually perceived by workers as an increase in the real wage. Together the fall in the real wage perceived by employers and the increase in labour supply offered by workers enable employment to increase from N_0 to N_1. There is an associated increase of output from Y_0 to Y_1. Thus the increase in aggregate demand leads to both a higher price level and a higher output. The aggregate supply curve is upward-sloping.

But remember that the increase in the supply of labour is brought about because workers only perceive the increase in money wages not the increase in prices. However the increase in prices will not go unnoticed by employees forever. It will be taken into account in future wage demands, and they will endeavour to restore the previous level of real wages. As the higher level of prices comes to be incorporated into wage demands, the perceived wage approaches the real wage and the quantity of labour offered contracts from N_1 to N_0. Equilibrium will be restored when the price rise is fully anticipated, at which point both employees and employers perceive the same real wage rate. This can only occur when the perceived wage equals the actual wage, thus restoring the former equilibrium in the labour market. The expansion in output induced by the stimulus to aggregate demand is brought about purely by workers being fooled into mistaking a rise in nominal wages for a rise in real wages. Since the mistaken expectations cannot persist, neither can the higher real output. Output and employment must necessarily return to their former levels. The only lasting effect of the boost to aggregate demand is an increase in the price level.

The above explanation depends crucially on the hypothesis that workers are slower to adjust to inflation than employers, and it has been criticised for this reason. We note that several similar models have been advanced;[1] all depend essentially on non-fulfilled expectations. *In this view of the world, aggregate demand policy can only cause deviations from the natural rate of employment by fooling somebody.* But rational economic men and women will not be fooled forever. Any increase in employment is bound to be temporary, and the only permanent beneficiary of an aggregate demand stimulus is the inflation rate.

Money Wages are Inflexible

Our demonstration above that the supply curve is vertical depended crucially on the assumption that nominal wages are flexible and adjust rapidly to any increase in the general level of prices. However, many economists believe that money (nominal) wages are determined institutionally, and that factors such as

[1] Several alternative hypotheses are carefully analysed by Cherry, Clawson and Dean (1981–2).

relativities and 'the living wage' play a much greater role than market forces in determining nominal wages. Therefore, wages are essentially exogenous to the macroeconomic model and can be regarded as fixed.

Figure 3.12 shows the derivation of the supply curve when money wages are regarded as fixed. For simplicity let us assume initially that the supply of labour is infinitely elastic. This means that the supply curve of labour is represented by vertical line in Figure 3.12. Let us further assume that there is an excess supply of labour at the prevailing wage rates. This means that the demand

FIGURE 3.12
The Derivation of Aggregate Supply when Money Wages are Fixed

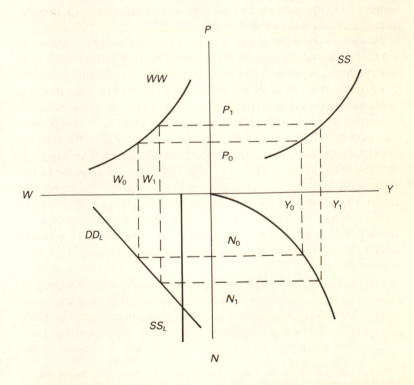

curve determines the quantity of labour employed. We shall relax these assumptions shortly. The fixed money wage W can be represented by a *rectangular hyperbola* in quadrant II.[1] Therefore, the curve WW denotes a fixed nominal wage. Along this curve WW the product of the two axes – the real wage and the price level – is constant.

Suppose that the economy is initially at output Y_0 and price level P_0. Employment is N_0 at a real wage rate w_0. Now suppose that the government boosts aggregate demand which raises the price level to P_1. The nominal wage remains fixed at W. From quadrant II, we see that this implies a fall in the real wage to w_1. The quantity of labour demanded increases to N_1, and since this is still less than the available supply, employment also increases to N_1. The higher price level P_1 is consistent with a higher level of output Y_1. If the price level is raised again, there will be a further increase in employment and output. In this way an upward-sloping aggregate supply curve is mapped out.

However, the institutions which determine money wages will probably respond in some way to the reduction in the real wage. We might expect some tendency for the wage level to be raised to restore the previous level of real wages. This will be manifest in a subsequent upward movement in the supply curve. If the nominal wage rises to offset fully the increase in the price level and restore the previous level of the real wage, output will return to its previous level also. This is illustrated in Figure 3.13, which repeats the essential features of Figure 3.12. Following an increase in the price level from P_0 to P_1, output increases. But now suppose that there is a subsequent increase in the nominal wage from WW_0 to WW_1. At the price level P_1 this is sufficient to restore the real wage to its previous level of w_0. This will be accompanied by a fall in output to Y_0. The increase in employment and output is only temporary.

But in this example where there is permanent excess supply of labour there is no mechanism which forces full adjustment of nominal wages to changes in the price level. It may well be that, although the economic expansion places upward pressure on the institutionally determined nominal wage, it fails to increase in the

[1] *Rectangular hyperbola* is the name given to the curve along which the product of the values of the two axes is constant. In this case the product of the real wage and prices, that is, the nominal wage, is fixed.

FIGURE 3.13
The Determination of Aggregate Supply Following Adjustment of the Money Wage

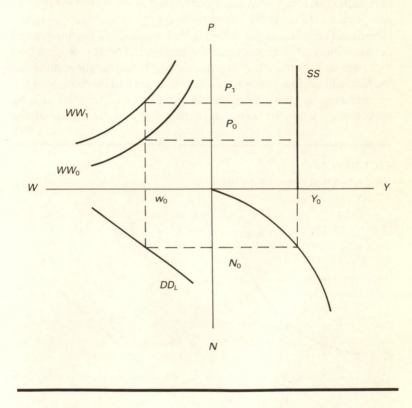

same degree as the increase in the price level. In this case, the subsequent rise in the nominal wage will lead to some reduction in output from the initial level of Y_1, but it will not fall as far as Y_0. In these circumstances, the aggregate supply curve has a permanent upward slope.

Let us now relax the simplifying assumptions of an infinitely elastic supply curve for labour coupled with permanent excess supply. Without these assumptions we have to be careful concerning the actual quantities traded when there is excess supply or demand. Consider for example the situation depicted in Figure 3.14 where the economy is stuck in an *underemployment equilibrium*. Equilibrium in the labour market would be achieved at an output level of Y_f (full employment) and price level P_0. For some reason the economy is currently operating at an output level of Y_1 and price level P_1. At the same time, there is excess supply in the labour market since at the existing real wage of w_1 the number of people willing to work exceeds the demand. The real wage is too high, but since nominal wages are rigid, the automatic equilibrating mechanism does not work. The real wage can be reduced if the aggregate price level is increased. This can be achieved by government action to boost aggregate demand. In terms of the

FIGURE 3.14
An Underemployment Equilibrium

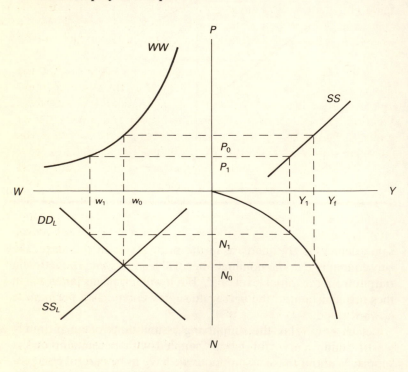

diagram, if the price level is increased to P_0, the real wage falls to w_0 restoring equilibrium in the labour market. Output is increased to Y_f, and the aggregate supply curve appears to be upward-sloping.

This is a highly simplified example of the fundamental economic problem addressed by Keynes. The economy suffers from high unemployment. One cause of the existing situation is that the real wage is too high, so that labour supply exceeds demand. For some reason the simple market adjustment of a fall in the nominal wage does not take place. There is no automatic tendency for the economy to restore full employment by itself. However, the government can bring about the necessary fall in the real wage by boosting aggregate demand thereby increasing the price level. The role of aggregate demand policy in this case is to overcome a market failure. We hasten to point out that, contrary to popular opinion, Keynes did not simply assume that money wages were rigid. He argued rather that individual employees and unions could not bring about a fall in the real wage unaided. For a discussion of this issue, we refer the reader to Addison and Burton (1982).

Finally, we note that it is not necessary to assume that the rigidity of wages applies equally to rises and falls. Indeed, there are some grounds for believing that wages are flexible in a upward direction but rigid downwards. It would seem that wage cuts are opposed vigorously by the union movement. In this case the aggregate supply curve will be kinked. This is illustrated in Figure 3.15. Assume as before that when the labour market is in equilibrium output equals Y_0 at the price level P_0. If the price level falls, the nominal wage rate remains at WW_0. Employment and output fall correspondingly. Below Y_0 then the aggregate supply curve is positively sloped. However, if the price level rises above P_0, the nominal wage rate increases accordingly. For example, if the price level rises to P_2, the nominal wage rate will rise to WW_2 so as to maintain the real wage. Employment and output remain unchanged. Therefore, for prices greater than P_0 the aggregate supply curve is a vertical line at Y_0.

In such a world, aggregate demand policy can operate effectively. For example, in Figure 3.16, if equilibrium is established at Y_0, P_0, the government can reduce output by restricting aggregate demand to DD_1. Conversely, if the economy is located at Y_1, P_1,

FIGURE 3.15
The Derivation of a Kinked Aggregate Supply Curve

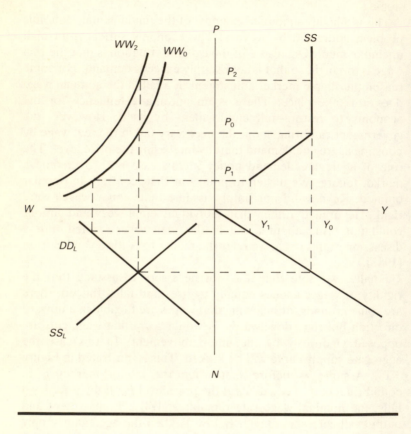

the government can increase employment by boosting aggregate demand to DD_0. But if the government attempts to increase employment still further beyond Y_0, it will be frustrated. Boosting aggregate demand from DD_0 to DD_2 only succeeds in increasing the price level.

We have now discussed two alternative rationalisations for the apparent positive slope of the aggregate supply curve. At this stage the two views do not appear to be very distinct. Both explanations depend upon a lag in the adjustment of the nominal wage to price

FIGURE 3.16
Effective Demand Policy with a Kinked Aggregate Supply Curve

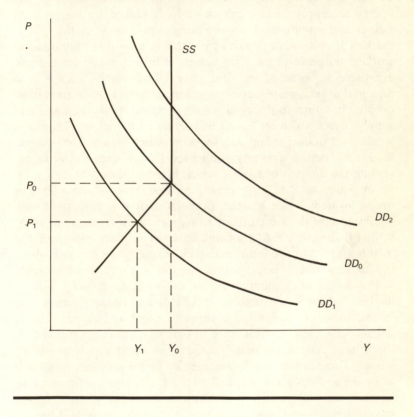

changes. In the first case, the lag arises because workers incorrectly perceive the true nature of the aggregate changes. In the second case, the lag in adjustment occurs because the nominal wage is determined institutionally. The difference is mainly one of degree. In the second case, the adjustment of money wages is much less automatic, the lags longer, and the adjustment possibly incomplete. Though they are seemingly minor and insignificant, we will see that these different conceptions have markedly different implications for efficacy of aggregate demand policy to manage the level of employment and output in the economy.

3.4   The Natural Rate of Unemployment

In the first of the explanations for the positive slope of the aggregate supply curve a special role is played by the level of output and employment representing equilibrium in the labour market. Employment departs from this equilibrium only because workers misperceive the true nature of an economic change and are therefore induced to alter their labour supply. Since it is argued that such misperceptions cannot persist, employment must eventually return to the equilibrium dictated by the demand and supply curves which are based on correct explanations. There is a single level of output and employment which is sustainable in the long run. There is a corresponding level of unemployment representing the amount of labour which is unemployed *at the equilibrium wage rate*. 'At any moment of time, there is some level of unemployment which has the property that it is consistent with equilibrium in the structure of *real* wage rates' (Friedman, 1968, p.8). Friedman dubbed this unique level of unemployment the '*natural rate*' and the term has stuck. Equally we can talk about the 'natural' rate of employment and the 'natural' rate of output.

The adjective 'natural' was an unfortunate choice, since it implies that there is something inevitable and righteous about the 'natural' rate of employment, unemployment and output. This is not the case. The 'natural' rate of employment is determined by the intersection of the demand curve for, and supply curve of, labour. These in turn are determined by factor supplies, tastes and technology. Nor is the 'natural' rate of employment immune to government policy. Any policy which succeeds in moving the labour demand and supply curves will alter the 'natural' rate.

Also unfortunate is the frequent tendency to equate the 'natural' rate of employment with 'full' employment. At the 'natural' rate of employment it is true that all who wish to work at the prevailing real wage rate are employed. But there may be a large pool of potential employees who would like to work but cannot find a 'suitable' job. Employment may fall far short of the available labour resources in the economy – resources which might be utilised by appropriate policies to shift the labour demand and supply curves. As one example, suitable tax policies might shift the demand and/or supply curves and in this wage move the 'natural' rate of employment closer to 'full' employment.

Furthermore, even 'full employment' does not mean 100 per cent employment. In any economy, there are always people changing jobs. There are people entering the labour market or returning to the labour market after a period outside, for example, for further education or to raise children. Such movements cannot be achieved instantaneously, and so at any point of time, there will be a certain percentage of the current labour force in transition and temporarily unemployed. This is termed *frictional unemployment*. Perceptions of the level of inevitable frictional unemployment have changed quite dramatically in recent years. In the United States in the 1960s a 4 per cent level of unemployment was accepted by the government as their full employment target. In Britain, frictional unemployment was regarded to be much lower. Over the period 1948 to 1968, unemployment in Britain averaged 1.6 per cent. In countries like Australia and New Zealand, the level of unemployment regarded as consistent with full employment was even lower. Today, many economists believe that the 'natural' rate of unemployment may be as high as 6 or even 8 per cent.

Does the concept of the 'natural' rate of unemployment apply also in the case in which the sloping aggregate supply curve is based upon an institutionally-determined real wage? Unfortunately the answer cannot be an unequivocal yes or no. In the sense that there is a single level of employment which is consistent with equilibrium in the labour market, the answer is yes. But since automatic market adjustments will not bring about equilibrium in the labour market in this world, the concept loses most of its force. We can define such a point but there is no necessary tendency for a market economy to converge towards it. It is not really a useful concept in such a world.

3.5 Inflation and Expectations

We have now seen how the government can use its control over aggregate demand to increase employment and output. But this is invariably accompanied by an increase in the price level. Indeed if the economy is at or near full employment it is possible that any boost in output will be temporary; after a period of adjustment the full impact of the increase in aggregate demand will fall on the price level. However, this is a once-and-for-all increase in the price level and not an inflation. Inflation requires a sustained and continuing rise in the price level. In this section we consider the relationship between aggregate demand policy and inflation.

Let us assume for the moment that wages and prices are flexible, but that workers are temporarily misled by any increase in economic activity. Assume further that the economy is initially in equilibrium at the 'natural' rate of employment. Suppose that this level of unemployment is politically unacceptable and that the government tries to reduce it by boosting aggregate demand. Initially, the policy will appear successful, with unemployment falling. But, as workers' expectations adjust to the new price level, their wage demands will rise, leading to an offsetting rise in unemployment. Eventually, the previous level of unemployment will be restored, at a substantially higher price level. However, if the government is determined to maintain a lower level of unemployment, it may stimulate aggregate demand once again, leading to another temporary decline in unemployment and a still higher price level. This is depicted in Figure 3.17. The true aggregate supply curve is represented by a vertical line at Y_N. Initially aggregate demand is represented by DD_0 and the economy is in equilibrium at E_0. The government increases aggregate demand to DD_1. Workers are initially fooled as to the true nature of the economic change and are induced to increase their supply of labour. The economy moves along the temporary supply curve SS_1. However, as workers' expectations accommodate the higher price level, they will reverse their increase in labour supply. The economy will gradually achieve a new equilibrium at E_2, with employment at the pre-existing level and higher prices. If the government once again increases aggregate demand, say to DD_2, the pattern will be repeated. The economy will first move along the temporary supply curve SS_2 to E_3 and then subsequently to E_4.

Of course, the government need not wait until the previous level of unemployment is restored (E_2) before once again stimulating aggregate demand. By repeated and continuing boosts to aggregate demand, it can maintain output and employment above the 'natural rate' indefinitely, but only at the cost of continuing inflation. In fact, by appropriate fine-tuning of aggregate demand, the government can maintain employment at the target level of Y_1

FIGURE 3.17
The Generation of Inflation

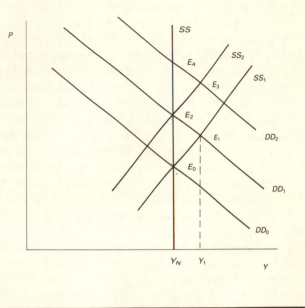

forever. Therefore, in the flexible price world, continuing inflation is thé necessary outcome of any government attempt to boost employment above the 'natural rate' by aggregate demand policy.

In the non-flexible-price world, inflation does not necessarily follow from aggregate demand policy to boost employment. There is no sharply defined 'natural rate', which is the only level of employment consistent with price stability. The ultimate impact of aggregate demand policy depends upon the response of wages to the resulting increase in prices and that is left unspecified in simple models since the money wage is exogenous. However, it is to be expected that any significant reduction in real wages brought about by aggregate demand expansion would put upward pressure on the nominal wage, leading to some reduction in the initial increase in employment. If the government attempts to offset this with further demand expansion, inflation is likely to result. Hence in this world inflation is not a necessary concomitant of government attempts to increase employment. However, if the government tries to maintain a level of employment which is 'too high', some inflation is likely to result. Again the difference between a world in which money wages are flexible and one in which they are not seems to be more a matter of degree than of kind.

At this point, we would like to recall our criticism of the behaviour underlying the cobweb model of expectations discussed in the previous chapter. There we remarked that naive hypothesis of expectations underlying the cobweb model seemed very inappropriate in a world of regular cobweb cycles. Similarly, the above discussion of inflation is based on a very similar expectations hypothesis. Workers are assumed to formulate their wage demands on the basis of the price level prevailing in the preceding period, which is analogous to the behaviour of producers in the cobweb model. After a long period of stable prices, this is a rational and appealing procedure. However, at a time of continuing inflation, it is as naive and unsatisfactory as the cobweb hypothesis.

If recent experience in the economy has been of price-inflation, workers will surely take that experience into account when formulating their wage demands. They will base their evaluation of nominal-wage offers on the prices which they expect to rule in the coming period, rather than the price prevailing in the preceding period. This has a profound effect on the process of inflation.

Figure 3.18 is similar to preceding figures, except that the vertical axis has been labelled with numerical values. Suppose that the economy has arrived at position E_0 with an inflation rate of 10 per cent. That is, over preceding years, output has been constant at Y_N with the price level increasing at 10 per cent per year. To achieve this, the government has had to expand nominal demand at 10 per cent per year to maintain the real level of aggregate demand. Similarly, the supply curve has shifted up a corresponding amount to offset the rise in price level. Now suppose that the government decides to stimulate employment by increasing aggregate demand at an annual rate of 20 per cent. Since only a 10 per cent rise in prices is expected, output will expand along the supply curve SS_1. The price level rises by more than 10 per cent, but less than 20 per cent. In Figure 3.18, this price rise is 15 per cent. However, expectations for the next period will be adjusted

FIGURE 3.18
Continuing Inflation

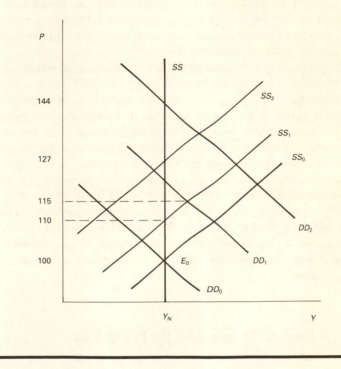

upwards to account for the unexpectedly high price rise. In this next period, then, aggregate demand will expand 20 per cent, while aggregate supply curve may rise 15 per cent. Again, there will be an unexpected price rise. Eventually, however, a 20 per cent inflation will come to be fully anticipated in the supply curve, whereupon output will return to its 'natural level' and both the supply and demand curves will rise upward at 20 per cent per year. The aggregate demand policy succeeds in attaining a temporary boost to employment, but the only lasting impact is a permanent increase in the rate of inflation.

What if the government is determined to maintain output above its 'natural' level? If prices and wages are flexible, output will exceed its 'natural' level only if expectations are wrong. Any given rate of demand expansion will eventually come to be fully anticipated, that is, incorporated into expectations. The only way in which a government in such a world can maintain a level of employment in excess of the 'natural' rate is continually to accelerate the expansion of aggregate demand, thereby generating a succession of expectational errors. A necessary concomitant of this activity is an accelerating inflation.

Therefore, when we introduce a more reasonable expectations hypothesis into a world of flexible wages, we find that not even a sustained inflation is capable of maintaining a level of employment in excess of the natural rate. The price for a higher than 'natural' level of employment is an accelerating inflation.[1] As before, if wages are less than completely flexible, the world is not as stark. Since the process of nominal-wage formation is regarded as exogenous, the mechanism of expectation-formation is not specified explicitly. However, presumably workers in this world are equally adept at taking expected price rises into account. Therefore, while there might be a band in which employment policies are successful, we might expect the pursuit of an employment target which was 'too high' to lead eventually to an accelerating rate of inflation.

3.6   Economic Targets and the Policy Rule

Consider once again the example which opened this chapter: driving a car into a garage. We said then that the target was to get the car inside. More precisely, the target is to manœuvre the car into a particular geographical location. But notice that the driver is probably not too fussy about the precise location of the car inside the garage. Although the driver may have a very precise target in mind, for example exactly in the middle of the garage, he will not consider that he has failed if he does not achieve this target precisely. There will be a satisfactory region around the target within which we will consider his goal has been achieved. The

---

[1] Perhaps the reader is tempted to ask what happens when workers come to anticipate the acceleration. This will become apparent in the next chapter.

FIGURE 3.19
Unemployment and Inflation as Targets of Economic Policy

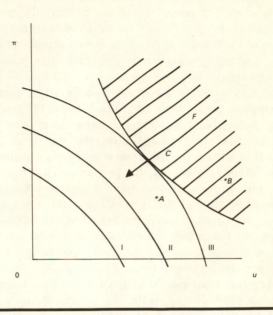

satisfactory region will allow sufficient room for getting into and out of the car, storing other equipment and so on.

The targets of macroeconomic policy are many: unemployment, inflation, interest rates, wages, economic growth, the balance of payments and so on. For the purposes of this book, we are especially concerned about two targets: the level of employment (unemployment) and the rate of inflation. Furthermore, like the position of the car, these targets are not precise numbers which must be achieved. Although the targets may be zero unemployment and zero inflation, these are not expected to be attained. Rather, less unemployment and less inflation will be preferred to more. The targets provide a means by which alternative feasible outcomes can be evaluated and the optimal chosen.

This is illustrated in Figure 3.19, which shows various combinations of unemployment (u) and inflation (π). The notional target is the origin with zero unemployment and zero inflation. Combinations of unemployment and inflation can be ranked according to their distance from the origin, and indifference contours such as I, II, III can be drawn. Outcome *A* is preferred to outcome *B*. If the region labelled *F* represents the set of feasible outcomes, the optimal policy choice is clearly the point of tangency between the boundary of the feasible set and the lowest attainable indifference contour – namely point *C*. In this case, the policy choice is straightforward.

Figure 3.19 presents an unrealistically static picture of the macroeconomic policy problem. In fact the set of feasible outcomes *F*, and perhaps also the targets, change from period to period. Moreover, they are dependent on the outcomes of previous periods. That is to say the macroeconomic policy problem is truly a dynamic, multi-period decision problem. This means that the optimal solution requires specifying a time-path for the available policy instruments and not just a value for a single year. For example, the solution may be expressed in terms of annual increments to the money supply over successive years. We shall call the solution of the policy problem, specifying a time path for each of the relevant *instruments*, a *policy rule*.

A policy rule may specify values for the instruments solely as functions of time. For example, the policy rule may specify that the money supply will be increased 10 per cent each year regardless of the current state of the economy. Such a solution is called a *passive* policy rule. Alternatively, the policy rule may be such that the optimal values of the instruments in any period depend upon the economic conditions in previous periods. This is called an *active* policy rule. An active policy rule allows feedback from the past to determine current policy; a passive rule has no such feedback. We shall give specific examples of both active and passive policy rules in the next chapter.[1]

At one time, there was considerable controversy in economics regarding the relative merits of active versus passive policy rules.

---

[1] The distinction between active and passive policy rules is analogous to the distinction in engineering between closed loop and open loop control. Traffic lights (signals) illustrate both types. Some traffic lights operate purely on a time-basis, shifting in regular and uniform sequence from green to red and back again. This is an open loop (passive) system. There are other traffic lights in which the sequence and duration of signals depends in part on the traffic at the time as measured by sensors embedded in the road.

It can easily be demonstrated that, under conditions of uncertainty, an active policy rule is superior to a passive policy rule. In spite of this, many economists, led by Milton Friedman, have argued in favour of a passive policy rule for monetary policy. Their case is based upon our lack of knowledge of the precise structure of the economic system and in particular on their belief that the lags between the setting of monetary policy and its impact on the economy are long and variable. This is really a further example of the long-running debate between the 'activists' and the 'passivists' which was mentioned in Chapter 1. Prior to the advent of rational expectations, the 'activists' appeared to be winning this particular aspect of the debate on points. Rational expectations theorists, however, claim to have made the debate irrelevant.

3.7 Conclusion

In this chapter, we have reviewed the mechanics of macroeconomic policy. The government has at its command an array of monetary and fiscal instruments such as the money supply and tax rates. By manipulating these instruments, the government can move the IS and LM curves, which in turn moves the aggregate demand curve. That is why we have labelled the process as a whole *aggregate demand management*. Changes in aggregate demand will have an impact on the level of employment, output and prices. The division of any change between output (employment) and prices depends on the slope of the aggregate supply curve. Provided that the supply curve is not vertical, the government can alter the level of employment (and unemployment) in the economy, albeit at the cost of some change in the price level.

Unfortunately, our theory tells us to expect the aggregate supply curve to be vertical if all prices and wages are flexible. This conflicts with observed fluctuations in the level of output and with the apparent past success of aggregate demand management. Two modifications to the theory are commonly used to overcome this conflict. In the first, the supply curve may depart from vertical because of errors in perceptions and expectations. Since such errors must be transitory, so is the slope of the supply curve. In the long run, the supply curve is vertical. The second modification involves the hypothesis that wages are determined institutionally and are slow to adjust to change in prices. This too imparts a potential slope to the aggregate supply curve and allows scope for aggregate demand policy. In practical terms the difference between these two views appears to be slight, involving the speed of adjustment. However, we shall see that the distinction becomes quite critical when we add the assumption that expectations are formed rationally.

Any aggregate demand policy which increase output and employment also inevitably increases the price level. That in itself does not constitute an inflation. However, repeated attempts to maintain employment above a level sustainable in the long run will lead to inflation and possibly to accelerating inflation. Macroeconomic policy then boils down to choosing a time-path for the available instruments so as to maximise the level of employment while at the same time minimising the level of inflation. Since these targets are conflicting, the optimal policy requires some trade-off between the targets. The time-path for the instruments is called *a policy rule*.

The trade-off between the policy goals unemployment and inflation is usually expressed in terms of the Phillips curve. In this chapter we have chosen to develop our exposition in terms of aggregate demand and supply, which means that we have focused on output and the price level rather than directly on unemployment and inflation. We discuss the Phillips curve in the appendix to this chapter.

In the previous chapter, we unreservedly dismissed the cobweb hypothesis as a reasonable representation of human behaviour in such markets. Earlier in this chapter, we pointed out that a very similar hypothesis was employed in macroeconomic theory. In fact, this naive view predominated in both theory and policy in the 1950s and 1960s. With hindsight, it is perhaps surprising that economists could have been satisfied with such an obviously deficient model of expectations formation. In their defence, we should point out that the period in question was one of mild and relatively stable inflation, in which the assumption of expectations based on the preceding periods price level was a very reasonable approximation. But the assumption became untenable in the late 1960s and the 1970s when the inflation rate became high, accelerating and variable.

Appendix: The Phillips Curve

In this chapter we discussed the effectiveness of demand management policies for controlling inflation and unemployment. Our discussion used the framework of aggregate supply and demand since this is the basis of most rational expectations models. However, much of the policy discussion and theoretical development in recent years has been conducted in a different conceptual framework, one known as the Phillips curve. Because of its important role in the development of macroeconomic thinking, we now tell the story of the rise and fall of the Phillips curve.

FIGURE 3A.1
Unemployment v. Rates of Change of Money Wages, United Kingdom 1862 to 1913

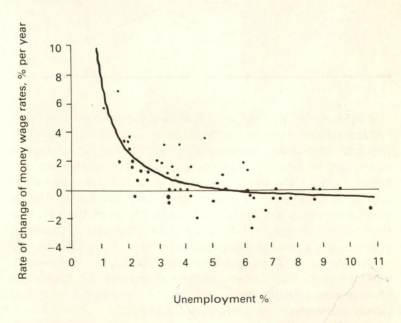

SOURCE   Phillips [1958]

FIGURE 3A.2
A Stylised Phillips Curve

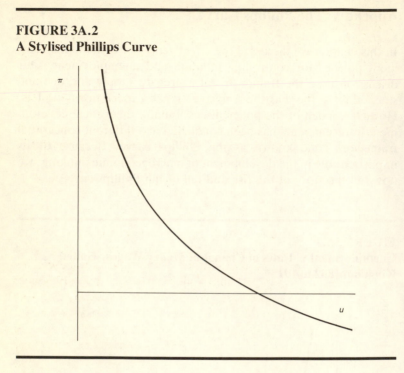

In 1958, A. W. K. Phillips, a New Zealand economist working in Britain, drew attention to the existence of a stable, long-term, empirical relationship between the rate of increase of money wages and the rate of unemployment. He showed that for one hundred years a low rate of unemployment had been associated with a rapid increase in money wages and vice versa. This is strikingly illustrated in Figure 3A.1, which is taken from Phillips (1958, p. 285). Figure 3A.1 depicts the percentage rate of change of money wages against the unemployment rate in the UK. for the years 1861 to 1913. Since low rates of unemployment usually implied high levels of demand for labour, and probably high levels of aggregate demand, this suggested that money wages rose rapidly when aggregate demand was historically high and slowly when it was low. Since money wages are a cost of production, this implied that there was a link between the rate of price increase and the level of unemployment. Thus the Phillips curve can be expressed as a relationship between the level of unemployment and the rate of inflation.[1]

A stylised Phillips curve is shown in Figure 3A.2 with inflation on the vertical axis and unemployment on the horizontal axis. Three features of this curve should be noted:

1. The curve has a negative slope with low unemployment associated with high inflation and vice versa.
2. The shape of the curve is markedly non-linear. Successive reductions in unemployment exact an increasing cost in terms of inflation.
3. The curve intersects the horizontal axis at a positive level of unemployment. This means that price stability (zero inflation) requires some positive level of unemployment.

The Phillips curve presented the policy-maker with an uncomfortable dilemma. The twin goals of zero unemployment and zero inflation were mutually inconsistent. There was a trade-off between unemployment and inflation, with lower unemployment being achievable only at the cost of higher inflation, and vice versa. Moreover, zero inflation could only be achieved at a level of unemployment that was socially and politically unacceptable. It was the lot of post-war industrial countries to suffer inflation and unemployment simultaneously. The Phillips curve then represented a 'menu' of policy choices open to the policy-maker. It would be expected that Conservative governments would choose points involving higher unemployment and lower inflation than Labour governments.

We can relate the Phillips curve to the aggregate demand and supply framework as follows. Assume once again that prices and wages are completely flexible, but that workers are temporarily fooled by any increase in money wages. Since in the short run there is a one-to-one correspondence between the level of output and the level of employment (Figure 3.5) and since the level of employment is inversely related to the level of unemployment, the axis of Figure 3.16 can be re-labelled using unemployment rather than output on the horizontal axis. Suppose the government

---

[1] It is not widely known that the empirical relationship between unemployment and inflation was first investigated by the American economist Irving Fisher (1926). However, he did not draw the eye-catching curve that has come to be associated with the name of Phillips.

FIGURE 3A.3
Unemployment and Inflation, UK 1955 to 1981

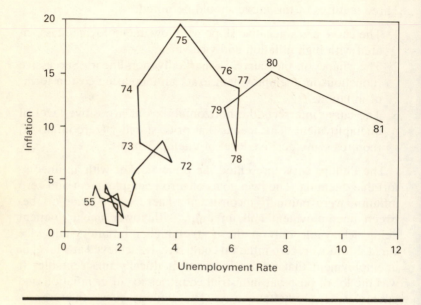

attempts to reduce the level of unemployment below the natural rate by boosting aggregate demand. If the reduction in unemployment is not to be temporary, the aggregate demand stimulus must be repeated in every period, resulting in a continuing rise in the price level. Furthermore, the lower the target rate of unemployment, the greater is the required boost in aggregate demand, the greater is the pressure on prices, and the higher the inflation. Therefore, for every target level of unemployment, there is a given rate of inflation; the lower the target level of unemployment, the higher is the resulting rate of inflation. The relationship between the target rate of unemployment and the resulting inflation traces out a Phillips curve. There is a single target level which is consistent with zero inflation – this is the ubiquitous 'natural' rate of unemployment.

The Phillips curve was a striking representation of the choice-set open to the policy-maker. Through the 1960s, work proceeded

FIGURE 3A.4
Unemployment and Inflation, USA 1955 to 1981

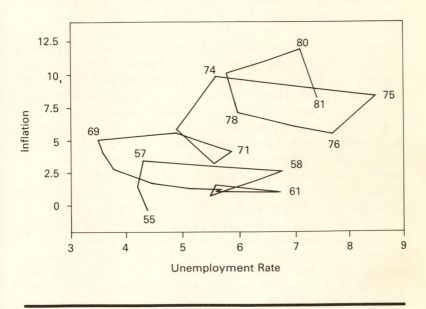

apace in estimating and re-estimating the Phillips curve for more
and more economies. Ingenious theoretical models were developed to explain the existence of the Phillips curve in terms of
individual maximising behaviour. The Phillips curve was the
backbone of unemployment and inflation policy in most Western
countries. It was a triumph for economics.

Sadly, however, as soon as the economics profession seemed to
have the Phillips curve pinned down and the policy-makers had
begun to exploit it in earnest, it began to shift. In the late 1960s in
both the UK and the US, increase in unemployment were associated with increases rather than decreases in unemployment. In
other words, the Phillips curve appeared to be shifting rapidly and
at an accelerating pace in a north-westerly direction, and exhibit-
ing a positive rather than a negative slope. This process is
illustrated in Figures 3A.3 and 3A.4 for the UK and US. The
phenomenon of 'stagflation' – the simultaneous occurence of high

inflation and high unemployment – dramatically upset the econo-mic conventional wisdom. It was a body blow to macroeconomics, from which it has yet to recover.

With hindsight, it is easy to see the fatal flaw in the Phillips curve rationale. For it is based on the same naive expectations hypothesis as the cobweb model. In our description above of the derivation of the Phillips curve from aggregate demand and supply analysis, it is implicity assumed that workers evaluate wage demands on the basis of the price level prevailing in the preceding period. In a period of high inflation, however, they will surely take into account expected price-rises in evaluating wage offers. There-fore, it is suggested, the position of the Phillips curve in unemploy-ment–inflation space depends upon expected inflation. The unique Phillips curve of Figure 3A.2 should be replaced by a family of curves, each curve corresponding to a different level of expected inflation.

This is illustrated in Figure 3A.5, which shows a family of Phillips curves, each indexed by a different level of expected inflation. Suppose the economy has been operating for some time at position E_0, with a long period of stable prices and an unemployment rate of 4 per cent. Suppose further that the government determines to reduce the level of unemployment by stimulating aggregate demand. Since expected inflation is zero, the government can choose any point along the curve L_1. Let us assume it moves the economy to point E_1. Unemployment is reduced to 2 per cent, but inflation for the year is now 2 per cent. The following year, the effective trade-off available to the govern-ment is given by L_2, since expected inflation for this year is now 2 per cent. If the government succeeds in maintaining unemploy-ment at 2 per cent for a further year, there will be 4 per cent inflation (point E_2). Taking this into account in the following year's expectations, the relevant trade-off is now L_4. An unem-ployment rate of 2 per cent can be achieved again (at point E_3) but at the cost of an inflation rate of 6 per cent.

We conclude from this model that the trade-off between unem-ployment and a given rate of inflation does not exist, except in the short run. Government policy can reduce the unemployment rate below the 'natural rate', but only at the cost of steadily increasing inflation. Furthermore, we note that even if demand policy is used to obtain a *temporary* reduction in unemployment, it will lead to a

FIGURE 3A.5
A Family of Phillips Curves

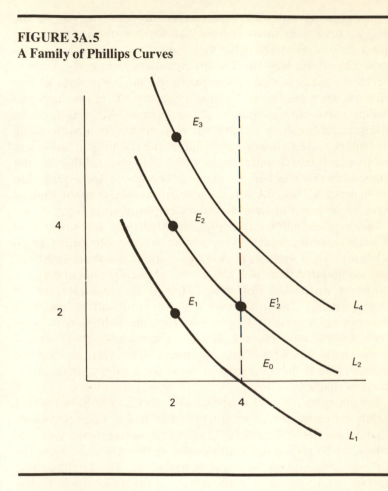

permanent increase in inflation. For example, if after moving the economy from E_0 to E_1, the government allows aggregate demand to fall in the subsequent period, restoring the previous unemployment level of 4 per cent, the economy does not return to E_0, but to E_2. In other words, the economy now inherits a permanent inflation rate of 2 per cent. So a further implication of this model is that, once a positive level of inflation has been established, restoration of price stability will require a period of unemployment in excess of the 'natural' state. Inflationary expectations have to be purged from the system.

Incorporating inflation expectations into our analysis of the Phillips curve transforms it from a stable long-term relationship into a short-term relationship valid only for given price expectations. The reason why the Phillips curve was apparently stable in the early studies is that it was measured during periods of low inflation, when prices were relatively constant. Thus the measured Phillips curve corresponds to L_0 in Figure 3A.5. As soon as governments began to exploit this relationship by moving along the Phillips curve to lower employment, the resulting inflation was incorporated into expectations, destroying the validity of the relationship that was being exploited. Therefore, one explanation for Figures 3A.3 and 3A.4 is the upward movement of the Phillips curve as the result of over-ambitious employment policy.[1]

The original Phillips curve suggested that there was single level of unemployment which is consistent with stable prices (zero inflation). When we incorporate expectations in a more satisfying way, we find that there is a single level of unemployment which is consistent with *stable inflation* – this is the 'natural rate' of unemployment. The observed apparent trade-off is purely a short-run phenomenon. In the long run, the Phillips curve (the locus of stable unemployment–inflation combinations) is vertical at the 'natural' rate of unemployment. The vertical long-run Phillips curve is the analogue of the vertical supply curve of the previous chapter.

The appendix has told a similar story to Chapter 3, but with a slightly different cast of characters. For it was unemployment, inflation and the Phillips curve, rather than aggregate demand and supply, which played the leading roles in the undermining of the post-war consensus on demand management. The Phillips curve represented the crowning achievement of the policy-advisers during the zenith of demand management in the 1960s. Alas, it also symbolised the rapid decline of macroeconomics's prestige, as it darted, twisted and turned during the 1970s. Its story is important

---

[1] The fate of the Phillips curve is reminiscent of the Heisenberg Uncertainty Principle in physics, which suggests that the very act of attempting to observe an atomic particle will cause it to change its location. Similarly, the attempt to exploit the trade-off suggested by the Phillips curve causes the trade-off to change. This was foreshadowed by Harry Johnson in 1963 when he wrote 'it may reasonably be doubted whether the (Phillips) curve would continue to hold its shape if an attempt were made by economic policy to pin the economy down to a point on it.' Johnson (1978a, p. 132).

to an understanding of the development of macroeconomic theory.

In Chapter 3 we presented two alternative schools of economic thought regarding the determination of wages and prices. For the first school, wages and prices are completely flexible, but economic agents may temporarily misperceive the true nature of a change in economic conditions. The second school dispenses with the complete flexibility of wages and prices, emphasising the institutional determination of wages rather than misperceptions as the cause of the sloping supply curve. We have analysed the Phillips curve from the viewpoint of the first school of thought which presents the issues starkly. For those economists who do not believe in market-determination of wages and prices the simple explanation of the Phillips curve was less convincing and many of this persuasion regarded the stable Phillips as little more than a statistical illusion (Trevithick, 1980, p. 61). More eclectic economists believe that the Phillips curve represented one important aspect of the inflationary process. Contrary to the flexible price school, however, they recognised that other factors were also important and these other factors (e.g. union militancy) could actually move the Phillips curve. Therefore, this second school should have been less surprised by the instability revealed in the 1970s. However, they were equally vulnerable to the problems of ignoring the impact of expectations.

In Chapter 3 we suggested that, if prices and wages were not flexible, there was no reason to think that the 'natural' rate of output was a unique point. The 'natural' rate of unemployment may be regarded as a range rather than a single point. Furthermore, admitting exogenous factors allows us to conceive of the long-run Phillips curve having a negative slope after all. Provided there is some inflexibility in prices and wages, there may be a permanent trade-off between unemployment and inflation.

One might suspect that the slope of the long-run Phillips curve was a simple, well-defined magnitude which could be measured empirically, and thus decisively distinguish between two competing paradigms of economics. Alas, economics is not so simple. Early empirical estimates of the slope of the long-run Phillips curve were significantly less than vertical. However, as inflation accelerated during the late 1960s and the 1970s, the estimated curve became steeper and steeper. With recent data, the hypothesis of a vertical long-run Phillips curve cannot be rejected (Gordon, 1976). Interpreting these results is compounded by the difficulties of trying to estimate the slope of a curve the position of which may be moving. Therefore, although the weight of evidence supports a non-vertical Phillips curve, it cannot be said to adjudicate decisively between the competing theories.[1]

[1] Mention was made earlier of Fisher's 'discovery' of a link between unemployment and inflation. It is interesting that Fisher suggested a direction of causality different from that proposed by Phillips. For he suggested that higher inflation would cause higher unemployment, rather than the other way around. This is precisely the interpretation of rational expectations theorists.

Rational Expectations: the Challenge to Policy

4

The significant impact that rational expectations models have made on economics in the last ten years is due principally to one result: namely, that aggregate demand management designed to lower unemployment will always be ineffective. In the previous chapter we discussed the conceptual background to demand – management policy. We showed how the government could alter the level of employment prevailing in the economy by manipulating the level of aggregate demand through its command of monetary and fiscal policy. However, we noted that if prices and wages were completely flexible, any departure from the natural level of employment was bound to be temporary. But rational expectations theorists go much further. They argue that such policy is ineffective even in the short run – 'an accurate understanding of how expectations are formed leads to the conclusion that short-run stabilisation policies are untenable' (McCallum, 1980). In other words, the government cannot systematically alter the level of employment, even in the short run, through monetary and fiscal policy. This is known as the *policy impotence* result of rational expectations. In this chapter, we show how policy impotence can be derived in a simple model which combines the hypotheses of expectations-based supply schedules and rational formation of those expectations.

We should perhaps signal in advance that an important line of criticism to the formulation below focuses on the nature of the supply curve. Critics suggest that the strong policy-impotence result flows principally from the unrealistic, restrictive form of the economic model employed. This point is developed further in the next chapter.

4.1   The Model

The policy impotence result of rational expectations can be illustrated with a simple model containing four ingredients. These include an aggregate demand equation, an aggregate supply equation, a requirement that expectations be formed rationally, and an equation to describe how the government formulates its policy. We begin by developing a mathematical expression of the aggregate demand and supply curves of Figure 3.6.

The demand curve of Figure 3.6 is simply a negative relationship between income (output) and the price level. This can be expressed as :

$$y_t = \alpha - \beta \, p_t$$

where

$$y_t = \text{income}$$
$$p_t = \text{price level}$$

However, the position of the demand curve depends upon monetary and fiscal policy and we want to allow for the impact of policy within the model. We can incorporate policy into the model by adding another variable x_t to represent a government policy instrument as follows:

$$y_t = \alpha x_t - \beta p_t \tag{4.1}$$

where

$$x_t = \text{the government policy instrument.}$$

We might think of x_t as the money supply or perhaps as a suitable composite of the policy instruments available to the government. The important point is that the level of x_t is under the direct control of the government. It can increase aggregate demand by raising x_t and vice versa. Graphically, equation (4.1) is a family of straight lines in price-output space, with the family indexed by x_t. Higher curves correspond to higher values of x_t.

The supply curves of Figure 3.6 may also be represented as a family of curves in price-output space. In this case, however, the curves are upward sloping and indexed by the expected price level. This family of curves can be expressed:

$$y_t = Y + \delta p_t - \delta p^*_t$$

where

p^*_t = the expected price level.
Y = the 'natural' rate of output.

We note two important properties of this equation.

● For given price expectations, there is a positive relationship between output and prices.
● If price expectations are realised $(p_t = p^*_t)$, then y_t equals Y.

What happens to the supply curve when price expectations change? Let us consider the example

$$y_t = 10 + 2p_t - 2p^*_t$$

and examine the effect of various expected price levels. This gives rise to the alternative supply curves reported in Table 4.1.

Table 4.1

p_t	y_t
1	$8 + 2p_t$
2	$6 + 2p_t$
3	$4 + 2p_t$

The alternative supply curves are depicted graphically in Figure 4.1. The expected price, p^*_t, serves as an index to the family of supply curves.

Clearly then the supply equation has the properties of the supply curve in Figure 3.4, namely:

●   For given price expectations, the aggregate supply curve is upward sloping. Moreover, the supply curve is shifted upwards when the expected price level increases.

●   If prices are exactly anticipated ($p_t = p^*_t$), the output (y_t) is equal to the natural rate of output (Y). Since we assume that expectational errors cannot persist, the long-run supply curve is vertical.

A perennial fact of economic life is uncertainty. To allow for uncertainty, we can enrich the model by adding a stochastic term (u_t) to supply function, as follows:

$$y_t = Y + \delta(p_t - p^*_t) + u_t \tag{4.2}$$

u_t is a random variable representing stochastic variations in supply. This is analogous to the procedure which we adopted in applying rational expectations to the cobweb model in Chapter 2.

The third ingredient of our model is a specification of the means in which expectations are formed. As discussed in Chapter 2, the rational expectations hypothesis asserts that expectations are derived from structural equations which determine the outcome of the model. The expected price-level in period t is equal to the mathematical expectation of the price-level within the model, given all the information available in period $t-1$. This can be expressed as:

$$p^*_t = E_{t-1}[p_t] \tag{4.3}$$

where $E_{t-1}[\ ]$ is the mathematical expectation conditional on the information available in period $t-1$ (see footnote on p. 30).

For the time being we shall leave the fourth equation, that of the government policy rule, unspecified. The first three equations of our model are thus:

$$y_t = \alpha x_t - \beta p_t \quad \text{(demand)} \tag{4.1}$$

$$y_t - \alpha x_t - y_t$$

FIGURE 4.1
Supply Curves of the Basic Model

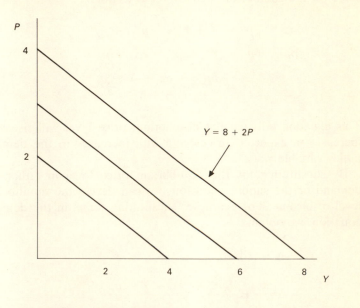

$$y_t = Y + \delta(p_t - p^*_t) + u_t \quad \text{(supply)} \quad (4.2)$$

$$p^*_t = E_{t-1}[p_t] \quad \text{(expectations)} \quad (4.3)$$

4.2 Solving the Model

In the previous section, we specified a simple macroeconomic model based on rational expectations. We want to use this model to analyse the effectiveness of demand-management policy when expectations are formed rationally. To do this, we must consider the impact on prices and output of changes in the government policy variable x_t.

The first step is to obtain the equilibrium level of output and prices for a given value of x_t. Equating demand and supply, we can solve for the equilibrium price level as follows:

$$\alpha x_t - \beta p_t = Y + \delta(p_t - p^*_t) + u_t$$

$$\beta p_t - \delta p_t = Y - \delta p^*_t - \alpha x_t + u_t$$

$$p_t = \frac{\delta p^*_t + \alpha x_t - Y - u_t}{\beta + \delta} \tag{4.4}$$

This equation tells us that equilibrium price level will rise with increases in expected prices and with increases in the demand policy variable x_t.

By substituting for the equilibrium price level in either the demand or the supply equation, we can derive the equilibrium level of income. For example, substituting for p_t in the demand equation, we obtain:

$$y_t = \alpha\, x_t - \beta\, p_t$$

$$= \alpha x_t - \beta\, \frac{\delta p^*_t + \alpha x_t - Y - u_t}{\beta + \delta}$$

$$= \frac{\beta Y + \alpha \delta x_t - \beta \delta p^*_t + \beta u_t}{\beta + \delta} \tag{4.5}$$

From this equation, we infer that higher price expectations lead to a reduction in output, whereas increases in aggregate demand increase output. These interpretations are what we would expect from our discussion in the previous chapter.

Equations (4.4) and (4.5) express p_t and y_t in terms of p^*_t and x_t. However, as we remarked in Chapter 2, p^*_t is not an operational variable. To close the model, we need to find an expression for p^*_t which involves only known quantities. This is the role of the hypothesis on expectations formation.

Equation (4.4) specifies the equilibrium behaviour of the price level for a given level of aggregate demand (x_t). The rational expectations hypothesis asserts that agents within the economy will use this equilibrium relationship to form their expectations. More precisely, the expected price level can be obtained by taking the mathematical expectations of equation (4.4). Remember that the *rational expectation* of price is based on all the information in the model and not just the past price information.

$$p^*_t = E_{t-1}[p_t]$$

$$= E_{t-1}\left(\frac{\delta p^*_t + \alpha x_t - Y - u_t}{\beta + \delta}\right)$$

$$= \frac{\delta E[p^*_t] + \alpha E[x_t] - E[Y] - E[u_t]}{\beta + \delta}$$

But

$$E[p^*_t] = p^*_t, \ E[Y] = Y, \ E[u_t] = 0$$

and therefore

$$p^*_t = \frac{\delta p^*_t + \alpha E[x_t] - Y}{\beta + \delta}$$

$$p^*_t = \frac{\alpha E[x_t] - Y}{\beta} \tag{4.6}$$

The rational expectation of the price level depends only on the 'natural' level of output and expected policy. We can use equation (4.6) to substitute for expected prices in equation (4.4) obtaining:[1]

$$p_t = \frac{\alpha \beta x_t + \alpha \delta E x_t - (\beta + \delta)Y - \beta u_t}{\beta(\beta + \delta)} \tag{4.7}$$

Then by subtracting equation (4.6) from equation (4.7) we can derive an expression for $p_t - p^*_t$, the price expectation error. This is the crucial term which determines the level of aggregate supply:

$$p_t - p^*_t = \frac{\alpha(x_t - Ex_t) - u_t}{\beta + \delta} \tag{4.8}$$

---

[1]When the intention is clear, we shall often drop the square brackets from the mathematical expectation operator E in order to avoid unnecessary notation. For example, we may write Ex_t in place of $E[x_t]$.

This equation tells us that rationally formed expectations of prices in period t will only differ from actual prices in period t (i) because of random factors (u_t) or (ii) because actual policy is different from expected policy. Substituting equation (4.8) into the aggregate supply equation (4.2), we obtain an expression for the aggregate level of output:

$$y_t - Y = \frac{\alpha\delta(x_t - Ex_t) + \beta u_t}{\beta + \delta} \tag{4.9}$$

The left-hand side of equation (4.9) measures the difference between the actual level of income and the natural rate. It might be loosely thought of as the level of unemployment. This equation implies output and employment can only deviate from their 'natural' rates for one of two reasons: (i) random variations in supply (u_t) or (ii) a departure of actual government policy from that expected ($x_t - Ex_t$).

There is an alternative derivation of equation (4.9). Equation (4.6) provides an expression for expected prices. This can be substituted directly into equation (4.5) yielding equation (4.9). This probably is a more usual derivation but it offers less insight.

4.3   The Policy Rule

From the previous section we know that, in a model of this type based on rational expectations, income will only deviate systematically from its 'natural' level if x_t differs from Ex_t – that is, if actual policy differs from its expected value. Some random variation in actual income arises from the u_t term in the supply function but this can not be an adequate basis for policy. Policy will be effective *if and only if* x_t systematically differs from Ex_t. This poses the questions: how is the policy level x_t determined and can it differ from Ex_t?

Recall from the previous chapter that the optimal solution to a policy problem can be expressed as a policy rule. It is a fundamental tenet of rational expectations theory that there exists a discernible policy rule determining government monetary and fiscal policy. The argument is simply that, unless policy is completely random, it will bear some systematic relationship to current and past values of economic variables. This systematic relationship can be discovered by observation and constitutes the policy rule. Furthermore it is in the interests of economic agents to determine the policy rule that currently governs economic policy.

The policy rule may in fact be a very complex function of a multitude of economic, social and political variables. For expository purposes, however, we shall consider some simple examples. Recall again the distinction between active and passive policy rules. An active policy rule is one in which policy in period t depends upon the performance of the economy in previous periods. By contrast, a passive policy rule is completely independent of recent economic performance.

An example of an active policy rule is:

$$x_t = k\, x_{t-1} + l\, y_{t-1} + mp_{t-1} \qquad (4.10)$$

Here, the level of the policy instrument in period t, x_t, is a function of income and prices in the previous period together with the policy decision of the previous period. In reality of course a policy rule might contain many other terms, such as current account deficits, unemployment rates, and so on.

By contrast, the rule:

$$x_t = k\, x_{t-1} \qquad (4.11)$$

is an example of a passive policy rule. If x_t is interpreted as the money supply, this is an expression of the z percent money growth-rate rule advocated by Milton Friedman. A passive rule might contain earlier values of the policy instrument (x_t, x_{t-1}) and many other variables, but it cannot depend upon any past state of the economy (y_{t-1}, p_{t-1}).

Of course, policy is seldom determined or implemented with the accuracy implicit in equations (4.10) and (4.11). We can allow for some random variation in the determination and implementation of policy by incorporating a random variable (v_t or w_t). For example, the active rule becomes

$$x_t = k\, x_{t-1} + l\, y_{t-1} + mp_{t-1} + v_t \qquad (4.12)$$

and the passive rule becomes

$$x_t = k\, x_{t-1} + w_t \tag{4.13}$$

Rational expectations theorists claim that there always exists some such expression of the policy rule, no matter how complicated the process of determining policy. Further, given sufficient experience, the form of the rule can be estimated by observation. Therefore, they assume, not only is government policy guided by such a rule but that the rule is known to all agents in the economy.

In the previous section we saw that deviations of output from its 'natural' level depend upon the difference between actual policy and its expected value. But the expected value of policy is determined by the policy rule. Treating the active policy rule first, we can take the expected value of equation (4.12) obtaining:

$$E(x_t) = k\, Ex_{t-1} + l\, Ey_{t-1} + m\, Ep_{t-1} + Ev_t$$

The expectation is conditional on the information available at $t-1$. Here we assume that the actual values of x_{t-1}, y_{t-1} and p_{t-1} are known. Therefore

$$Ex_{t-1} = x_{t-1}$$
$$Ey_{t-1} = y_{t-1}$$
$$Ep_{t-1} = p_{t-1}$$

Furthermore

$$Ev_t = 0$$

implying that

$$Ex_t = k\, x_{t-1} + l\, y_{t-1} + m\, p_{t-1} \tag{4.14}$$

This is, the expected policy in period t depends solely upon the values of the level of output, prices and policy in the previous period. Subtracting (4.14) from (4.12) we obtain:

$$x_t - Ex_t = v_t$$

Substituting this back into (4.9), we get another expression for the difference between actual and 'natural' output:

$$y_t - Y = \frac{\alpha\delta v_t + \beta u_t}{\beta + \delta} \qquad (4.15)$$

Since v_t and u_t are both random variables, the deviation of output from its 'natural' level is entirely random – systematic policy can have no influence in this model.

The expected value of the passive policy rule is:

$$Ex_t = k \, Ex_{t-1} + Ew_t$$

But

$$Ex_{t-1} = x_{t-1}$$

and

$$Ew_t = 0$$

Therefore

$$Ex_t = kx_{t-1}$$

and substituting this into (4.13), we get

$$x_t - Ex_t = w_t$$

and substituting this into (4.9) yields:

$$y_t - Y = \frac{\alpha\delta w_t + \beta u_t}{\beta + \delta} \qquad (4.16)$$

In this case also, any deviation of output from its 'natural' level is purely random. No systematic policy governed by a passive policy rule will have have any effect.

A careful analysis of these derivations will reveal that they do *not* depend essentially on the particular form of the policy rules. Although we used simple policy rules for expository purposes, the conclusions extend to all policy rules, no matter how complicated. The argument depends only on the simple observation that, for any policy rule, any deviation of actual policy from its expected value must be due to random variation. There can be no systematic variation.

This is the fundamental conclusion of rational expectations, namely that *in this class of model, no policy rule can have any systematic effect on the deviation of output from its 'natural' level.* The distinction between short-run and long-run effectiveness is irrelevant. Within the model, any systematic policy is completely impotent.

It is important to note that we have *not* demonstrated that policy has no impact on economic outcomes. Within the model, output is not identically equal to its 'natural' level. Random deviations are expected. Different policy rules will have different random error terms and thus contribute differently to the total variance of output. It should also be clear that within the model active and passive policy rules are equally impotent, although they may have different impacts on the total variance.

4.4   Would Adaptive Expectations Make any Difference?

To understand the role of rational expectations in the above results, it is useful to consider the same economic model where expectations are formed adaptively. As discussed in Chapter 2, *adaptive expectations* can be expressed as:

$$p^*_t = p^*_{t-1} + \eta(p_{t-1} - p^*_{t-1})$$
$$= \eta p_{t-1} + (1-\eta)p^*_{t-1}$$

Substituting this expression for expected prices into equation (4.5), we derive the following expression for the equilibrium level of income:

$$y_t = \frac{\beta Y + \alpha\delta x_t - \beta\delta\eta p_{t-1} - \beta\delta(1-\eta)p^*_{t-1} + \beta u_t}{\beta + \delta}$$

Since the only contemporaneous (current period) terms in this equation are x_t and u_t, we can conclude that current policy can systematically alter the actual level of output.

This can be made clearer by recalling from Chapter 2 that an adaptive expectations mechanism can be expressed as a distributed lag of all past prices, that is:

$$p^*_t = \eta \sum_{k=1}^{\infty} (1 - \eta)^{k-1} p_{t-k} \qquad (4.17)$$

Let us denote this weighted sum of all past prices as P_{t-1}. Then, with adaptive expectations, the equilibrium level of income in any period is given by:

$$y_t = \frac{\beta Y + \alpha \delta x_t - \beta \delta P_{t-1} + \beta u_t}{\beta + \delta} \qquad (4.18)$$

Now, in any period t, P_{t-1} depends only on past information – it is predetermined. Therefore, for given P_{t-1}, output y depends directly on policy x. In this way government policy is effective. It can systematically alter the level of output.

It is a property of adaptive expectations that when prices are stable the expected price will gradually converge to the real price. Therefore, a once and for all change in policy will not lead to a permanent change in output. However a permanent change can be achieved if expectations are prevented from ever 'catching up' with actual prices.

The reader will now see that the assumption of adaptive expectations was implicit in the discussion of the effectiveness of demand management and the slope of the supply curve in the previous chapter. Adaptive expectations enables effective policy in the short run, even in a model where policy is always ineffective with rational expectations. However, policy will not be effective in the long run unless policies are continually innovative.

4.5 Conclusion

The impact of rational expectations in economics is largely due to a simple proposition: *systematic aggregate demand policy can never be effective if expectations are formed rationally.* In this chapter, we have demonstrated the derivation of this proposition within a simple model. We have also shown that it depends essentially on the assumption of rational expectations. Policy is effective in the same model when expectations are formed adaptively.

But rational expectations is not sufficient for policy impotence.

Our derivation depends essentially on an economic model in which prices are completely flexible and the aggregate supply curve is vertical except for transient expectational errors. When complications such as rigid prices, capital markets and taxation are added to the model, different conclusions are obtained. One of the points which we would most like to emphasise is that the proposition of policy impotence is peculiar to a very special and limited class of economic model. The significance of this result is the topic of the next chapter.

The Counter-Attack 5

Many of the important advances in economic knowledge arise from confrontations. The Great Depression posed a fundamental challenge to the then prevailing conventional wisdom of the self-equilibrating economy. It refused to go away. Into this environment, Keynes introduced a radically different theoretical perspective, which threatened many cherished notions of the economics profession. His contribution was not greeted with universal acclaim and a counter-attack was mounted with vigour. The theoretical fundamentals of the *General Theory* were carefully examined and debated. New lines of empirical research were spawned. In response, Keynes and his followers were forced to amend, clarify and adapt the theory. The publication of the *General Theory* provoked a flurry of activity in macroeconomics, a thorough reassessment of both theory and evidence, and quite novel lines of research. Gradually, out of all this activity there emerged a new consensus founded on a much deeper and more thorough knowledge of macroeconomics.

Among other things, the consensus held that full employment was an identifiable and desirable goal. Governments had both the means and the responsibility to manage the economy in such a way as to achieve full employment, subject to an acceptable level of inflation. The necessary trade-off between unemployment and inflation was embodied in the Phillips curve. There was an acknowledged diversity of opinion on the best means of achieving any desired point on the curve and a corresponding diversity regarding the location of the optimum point. Both matters were regarded as legitimate aspects of government policy.

By the early 1970s, this consensus too was under attack from an unco-operative reality. Contrary to the negative trade-off implied by the Phillips curve, most Western economies were experiencing simultaneously high unemployment and high inflation. Conventional economic policies appeared powerless. Macroeconomics was again at a low ebb. Along came a new body of theory which purported to show that the traditional demand-management policies must of necessity be powerless. It was bound to have an impact.

We believe that the incorporation of rational expectations into macroeconomics was not serendipitous. Muth's seminal article introducing the notion of rational expectations was published in 1961. But it was not until a decade later, when the prevailing Keynesian orthodoxy was apparently unable to explain the then current economic conditions, that the idea was incorporated into macroeconomic theory. Like the *General Theory,* it was a radically new perspective which undermined some very cherished notions of the economics' profession. Like the *General Theory*, it stimulated a rash of research along novel lines, revitalising macroeconomic theory and practice. In short, it provoked a confrontation.

The debate about the rationality of expectations, its treatment in theory and its implications for policy still continues. Initial disbelief has been gradually transformed into a grudging acceptance of certain of the propositions emerging from rational expectations theory, while some of the more extreme claims of the proponents have been discredited.

In the remaining chapters of this book, we consider this continuing debate. We would like to show that the notion that expectations are formed rationally is a creative influence which has stimulated many new avenues of inquiry in economics. We would like to suggest that rational expectations has be too closely identified with an extreme 'classical' view of the economy from which it should herewith be divorced. Finally, we hope to indicate some of the positive avenues revealed by rational expectations which remain to be more fully explored.

The division of material between this chapter and the one which follows is somewhat imprecise. In Chapter 6, we focus on empirical studies which have been explicity designed to test the rational expectations hypothesis and its implications. This chapter, on the other hand, relates to criticisms which have been levelled at the theory on grounds of realism or consistency and at its ability to explain the stylised facts of economic history.

Of necessity, this chapter is more narrative than others in the book. In subsequent sections, we present a number of criticisms which have been made of rational expectations macroeconomcis; examine the responses to these criticisms of the proponents of rational expectations, then the responses to the responses and so on. It is a bit like trying to describe the ebb and flow of a military campaign. We therefore warn the reader that she (or he) may have to exert a little more effort than usual to maintain the thread of our presentation.

5.1   Rational Expectations are too Implausible

The first and most basic criticism thrown at rational expectations is that it is unrealistic to assert that individuals' expectations are 'essentially the same as the predictions of the relevant economic theory' (Muth, 1961, p316). This apparently requires that individuals know not only the past history of all the relevant variables, but also the structural parameters of the 'true' economic model. Further, they must engage in a prodigious amount of processing of this information, presumably by mental arithmetic. Since economists have so much difficulty in understanding and predicting economic behaviour, what sense does it make to assert that the average 'man or woman in the street' can do so without systematic error? Where do they acquire all this information? The appeal of adaptive and extrapolative expectations mechanisms was that they provided simple rules which people could follow in making predictions. In contrast, forming rational expectations places seemingly unreasonable demands on individual knowledge and processing power. It is simply not credible!

Note that one view of economic methodology would simply rule this criticism out of order, for the criticism questions the reality of assumptions. According to this view, the realism of assumptions is irrelevant. The only criterion by which to evaluate the scientific worth of a theory is its ability to predict Friedman (1953). If you are of this school, then please proceed directly to the next section, or perhaps the next chapter.

Fortunately, proponents of rational expectations have not universally adopted this defence and some have attempted to fight for rational expectations on its own ground. The following defences have been made.

Individuals are rational

Neoclassical economics is essentially concerned with trying to explain economic behaviour in terms of individual utility-maximising. How should any self-respecting utility-maximiser attempt to predict the values of unknown economic variables essential to his decisions? Rationally, of course. Rational expectations therefore is nothing more than the consistent application of neoclassical economic analysis to the decision-making under uncertainty. Therefore it should be beyond reproach. So say the proponents.

But rational expectations is not merely a proposition about the way in which economic agents use the available information. It also embodies a specific hypothesis about the available set of information; namely, individuals must have available information sufficient to enable them to form expectations which are identical to predictions of the relevant economic theory. Few economists would convincingly argue that individuals do not efficiently utilise the information available. However, it is a very different proposition to believe that the information requirements of rational expectations are met.

Further, to believe that individuals will use *efficiently* all the information available *does not* require that they incorporate all publicly available information in their decisions. Information-gathering and processing is costly. A rational individual will gather and process information up to the point at which the marginal cost of additional information is equal to its marginal benefit. Since the marginal cost is positive, it is likely that a rational individual will stop short of gathering all the publicly available information. If they do not use all the available information, it is possible for them to be systematically wrong in their expectations. This in turn allows for effective government demand-management policy.

Let us elaborate on the preceding point by referring back to the model analysed in the previous chapter. There, we derived the following expression for the deviation of output from its natural level:

$$y_t - Y = \frac{\alpha\delta(x_t - Ex_t) + \beta u_t}{\beta + \delta} \tag{5.1}$$

Let us assume that x_t is determined according to the policy rule:

$$x_t = kx_{t-1} + ly_{t-1} + mp_{t-1} + v_t \tag{5.2}$$

where

$$E[v_t] = 0$$

Under the assumption of rational expectations, the variables x_{t-1}, y_{t-1} and p_{t-1} and the parameters of the policy rule (k, l, m) will be known to all the market participants. In other words, they will be contained in the information set I_{t-1}. Therefore

$$E[x_t:I_{t-1}] = kx_{t-1} + ly_{t-1} + mp_{t-1} + E[v_t]$$
$$= kx_{t-1} + ly_{t-1} + mp_{t-1}$$

so that

$$x_t - E[x_t] = v_t \tag{5.3}$$

and equation (5.1) reduces to

$$y_t - Y = \frac{\alpha\delta v_t + \beta u_t}{\beta + \delta} \tag{5.4}$$

The only deviation of y_t from its natural level Y is due to the random error terms u_t and v_t. Government policy x_t has no systematic impact.

Consider now how this account is modified if x_{t-1} is not contained in the information set I_{t-1}; that is, if economic agents are not aware of the previous level of policy when they form their expectations of current policy. How would they form their expectation of x_t? Rationally, which means by taking the mathematical expectation of (5.2), namely

$$E[x_t:I_{t-1}] = kE[x_{t-1} : I_{t-1}] + ly_{t-1} + mp_{t-1}$$

and

$$x_t - E[x_t : I_{t-1}] = k(x_{t-1} - E[x_{t-1} : I_{t-1}]) + v_t$$

At first sight, it might seem as though we have just pushed the problem one step further back. But notice that Ex_{t-1} depends upon the value of x_{t-2}, which is included in the information set I_{t-1}. That is:

$$E[x_{t-1} : I_{t-1}] = kx_{t-2} + ly_{t-2} + mp_{t-2}$$

and

$$x_{t-1} - E[x_{t-1} : I_{t-1}] = v_{t-1}$$

Therefore, substituting this into the previous equation, we obtain

$$x_t - Ex_t = v_t + kv_{t-1} \tag{5.5}$$

Not surprisingly, the expectation error is larger when some information is missing. This can be seen by comparing equations (5.3) and (5.5). But the error remains entirely random. That is, even when individuals do not know the value of x_{t-1} when they form their expectation of x_t, their expectation error is a random variable. Lack of knowledge about one of the relevant economic variables *does not* in this case provide any scope for policy.

To emphasise this point we can substitute equation (5.5) into equation (5.1), obtaining:

$$y_t - Y = \frac{\alpha\delta(v_t + kv_{t-1}) + \beta u_t}{\beta + \delta}$$

Comparing this equation with equation (5.4), we see that the deviations of output from its natural rate will be greater when x_{t-1} is unknown at time t. But, though larger, the deviations are still random. There is no scope for policy.

By way of contrast, consider now the case in which individuals do not know the true value of the parameter k in the policy rule. Let us assume that the parameter is perceived to have the value k'. Then expectations of x_t will be formed according to

$$E[x_t : I_{t-1}] = k'x_{t-1} + ly_{t-1} + mp_{t-1}$$

whereas the true process governing evolution of policy is

$$x_t = kx_{t-1} + ly_{t-1} + mp_{t-1} + v_t$$

and

$$x_t - Ex_t = (k - k') x_{t-1} + v_t$$

When the true value of a parameter is unknown, expectation errors are not random. In fact, the expectation error is directly proportional to past policy. Substituting the previous equation into equation (5.1), we obtain:

$$y_t - Y = - \frac{\alpha\delta((k - k') x_{t-1} + v_t) + \beta u_t}{\beta + \delta}$$

In this case, deviations of output from its natural level are not entirely random. Instead they are systematically related to the level of policy in the previous period. We conclude that, if individuals do not know the parameters of the policy rule in our model, demand-management policy can be effective.

By way of a general conclusion, the non-availability or incorrectness of information does not necessarily imply that expectations are biased. However, some information failures will lead to a systematic bias in expectations, which may be exploited by government policy to alter the level of demand. Therefore, the information availability assumptions are crucial to the validity of the impotence of policy result of rational expectations.

Proponents of rational expectations have some further responses to criticism of the information availability assumptions.

The honest government argument

We have just seen the importance of the parameters of the government policy rule being correctly perceived. Proponents argue that a government interested in stabilising the economy has an incentive to reveal its true policy rule to the public. It seems plausible that a government wishing to stabilise the economy at the natural rate of unemployment would have an incentive to reveal its policy rule if it believed that expectations are formed rationally. But if the natural rate of unemployment is 5, 6 or even 7 per cent, the government may have no desire at all to stabilise at that level. Instead, it may wish to use demand management to lower the rate of unemployment below the natural rate (especially with the approach of an election). In this case, it will have an incentive not to reveal its true policy rule.

In our example, the parameters of the policy rule are prominent. In the real world, however, there are hundreds of relevant parameters, misperceptions of any one of which could give rise to the opportunity for effective policy. Of course, any scope for policy resulting from small errors in perceived parameters may be quantitatively unimportant.

All profit opportunities will be exploited

Expectation errors give rise to profit opportunities. In other words, agents with accurate expectations will be able to profit at the expense of those whose expectations are wrong. There are therefore strong incentives to 'get it right'. Economic agents will respond to those incentives and develop the correct expectations.

This response begs the question of how these agents 'get it right'. True, there are strong incentives to have accurate expectations. Most economists would agree that mistaken expectations cannot persist for long. This was nicely expressed by Keynes, when he wrote:

> **actions based on inaccurate anticipations will not long survive experiences of a contrary character, so that the facts will soon override anticipation except where they agree.** (Keynes, 1930, p. 160).

Proponents of rational expectations take this line of thought one step further and argue that such misperceptions will not even exist.

Only a subset need be rational

A slight variant of the preceding argument concedes that all the agents in the economy may not have rational expectations. In their view, it is sufficient if a few agents have rational expectations. These 'rational' agents will exploit their information advantage by trading with the ill-informed. Such profit opportunities will not be eliminated until the market expectation is rational. Thus, provided a subset of traders are rational, the market as whole will appear *as if* all participants had rational expectations.

No competing theories

The final response of the proponents of rational expectations is quite disarming: there are no competing theories with a similar claim to theoretical consistency and rigour. Unfortunately, this cannot be denied. Adaptive expectations and similar mechanisms are essentially *ad hoc* and arbitrary, and are not grounded in explicit maximising behaviour. However, this response assumes that a utility maximising explanation of any economic behaviour is *a priori* better, whereas it may be the case that a vague and subjective process such as expectation formation is better modelled as an adaptive, satisficing activity. The fact that there are no competing theories should not be used to justify the more extreme claims of the rational expectations theorists. Rather, it should be taken as a challenge to the ingenuity of economists to provide more adequate alternatives.

5.2 Learning to be Rational

A more subtle criticism of rational expectations theory concerns the process of achieving a rational expectations equilibrium. If human beings are not born with a comprehensive knowledge of the economy, how do they acquire it? Have expectations always been rational? What happens when the structure of the economy changes? How do agents acquire their knowledge of the new structure and what happens to expectations in the interim? If a rational expectations equilibrium exists, will it be attained by utility-maximising individuals?

The fundamental problem posed here is that rational expectations theory describes an equilibrium set of expectations. It has nothing to say about how that equilibrium set of expectations is attained. How does a rational expectations equilibrium become established in a real-world market? Unless we are prepared to assume that a rational expectations equilibrium has always existed, we have to consider the process by which the equilibrium is achieved. Presumably, convergence to an equilibrium is achieved by a process in which agents learn from their errors and adjust their expectations mechanism accordingly. Two problems can be identified in such a learning process:[1]

● Since the evolution of the system depends upon actual expectations, any agent needs to know how all the other agents are forming their expectations if he is to be able to make an unbiased forecast. If the rational expectations equilibrium has been established, he can assume that other agents are forming their expectations rationally, but if the equilibrium has not yet been established, what is he to assume about the other agents?

● Even if we assume that all the agents act identically and that a rational expectations equilibrium exists, 'there is no guarantee that actual economic agents will ever be able to discover it' (De Canio, 1979, p. 54). In other words, the agents may adopt a learning strategy which does not converge to the rational expectations equilibrium.

Shiller (1978) and De Canio (1979) present simple models in which economic agents learn the appropriate rational forecasting rule by means of a simple adaptive process. They show that this learning process will not converge to the rational rule unless a

---

[1]There is another related problem which deserves a mention here. Since rational expectations for this period depend upon estimates of the future while the future depends in part upon present expectations, there need be no unique rational expectation for the current period. Rather, there may be several rational expectations equilibria. What determines which equilibrium will be achieved?

certain stability condition holds. One might debate the significance of this result. On the one hand, perhaps there is another *ad hoc* learning process which would converge – we have just not modelled the process properly. On the other hand, it does seem that any mechanism for modifying expectations must be adaptive in some sense and hence open to the possibility that it will diverge from, rather than converge to, the rational expectations solution. These results do indicate that the problem of convergence is a serious one if we are to regard rational expectations being actually applied by 'flesh and blood' human beings. It is one of the areas in which further research is badly needed. Unfortunately, it is also a difficult problem to analyse.

Even a convergent process may take a significant time to converge. This must necessarily be the case if agents are to learn about the change by observing the behaviour of the economy. For example, suppose that the government changes its policy rule (or perhaps a new government is elected). Many periods will need to be observed in order to make a reasonably accurate estimate of the new rule. Several more periods must elapse in order to estimate the effect of the new rule on economic behaviour. Before the new equilibrium is reached, another change may come along (for example, another change of government) so that yet a different equilibrium must be sought.

> Even if a model does eventually converge on a rational expectations equilibrium, it may take such a long time to do so that, since the structure of the economy changes occasionally, the economy is never close to a rational expectations equilibrium. (Shiller, 1978, p. 39)

Moreover, during the process of convergence, expectations will be biased. During this transition process, demand-management policy will be effective (Taylor, 1975). If the convergence process is slow, the impotence of policy result is of little significance, since the economy is always in transition from one rational expectations equilibrium to another.

Do you get a feeling of *déjà vu*? This seems very reminiscent of the distinction between long-run and short-run policy effectiveness which has long been a topic for concern in macroeconomics. Prior to the advent of rational expectations, many if not most macroeconomists would have accepted a view of world in which demand-management could be effective in the short run but not in the long run. In the long run, the supply curve is vertical. But also, 'in the long run, we are all dead' (Keynes, 1964).

Some proponents of rational expectations have countered by arguing that there are never really any changes in policy rules or in the structure of the economy. All is predetermined and what is observed is merely the working out of different manifestations of the underlying structure of the economy. [1] When we observe what appears to be a change in structure, it merely indicates that we have not modelled the process adequately. Once again, this response begs the question of how the agents in the economy come to learn the details of this underlying structure. Are we born with a complete specification of the stochastic processes governing the economy?

5.3   The Economic Model is Wrong

As we have already stressed, the economic model underlying the impotence result is very special indeed. In this model, the aggregate supply curve is vertical at the natural level of output. The only departure from the 'natural' level of output and employment comes about from expectational errors – 'all unemployment is a voluntary, fleeting response to transitory misperceptions' (Modigliani, 1977, p.6).

The most fundamental and most damaging criticism which has been levelled against this model concerns its assumption of flexible prices and continuous market clearing. Critics argue that because of the widespread and obvious prevalence of contracts, explicit and implicit, and the prevalence of quantity rather than price adjustment in markets, the assumption of continuous market clearing embodied in the rational expectations models is clearly unsuitable.

A second line of attack levelled against this simplified economic model focuses on the failure adequately to model capital, inventories, wealth effects and so on. It cn readily be shown that anticipated monetary policy is no longer neutral when assets are

---

[1]By predetermined, we do not mean that the economy is non-stochastic. Rather, that the stochastic processes governing the ecoomy are given and unchanging.

incorporated in the model. In a related vein, the models have been criticised for not taking into account such real world institutions as taxation. We will consider each of these in turn.

It should also be noted that the basic impotence-result relates only to monetary policy. Fiscal policy, to the extent that it is effective, will be effective despite rational expectations. No one denies that the government is able to alter the natural rate of unemployment through certain types of fiscal policy. The basic impotence result, however, has often been portrayed as ruling out 'stabilisation policy' and not purely monetary policy. For example, McCallum writes 'An accurate understanding of how expectations are formed leads to the conclusion that short-run stabilisation policies are untenable' (McCallum, 1980, p. 37). This statement must be regarded as hyperbole.

Continuous market clearing

One of the objectives of the economists pioneering the application of rational expectations to macroeconomics has been to provide a rigorous conceptual foundation based on individual optimising behaviour. [1] A fundamental plank of this conceptual foundation is the belief that all markets clear instantaneously. By this we mean that it is assumed that supply is equal to demand in all markets at all times. It is further assumed that this equation of supply and demand is brought about by price adjustments. In other words, it is assumed that the Walrasian view of the world as a collection of auction markets overseen by an omnipotent auctioneer is most appropriate to the analysis and consideration of macroeconomic phenomena.

It is surely here that the theory, and in particular the impotence result, is most vulnerable. For the image of instantly-clearing auction markets is clearly and obviously at variance with even the most casual observation of the world about us. Inventories, queues, backlogs all belie the existence of clearing markets. The first reaction of buyers and sellers in many, if not most, markets is to adjust quantity rather than price (Akerlof, 1979; Okun, 1981).

[1]Later, we will have something to say about (i) whether this is a desirable goal and (ii) whether they have been successful in this quest.

We believe that people (economists excepted perhaps) hold and believe in notions of fairness in market-dealing. It is widely regarded as unfair to take advantage of a temporary shortage in a given commodity. Most transactions are not single instances; rather they are part of a continuing relationship between the buyer and seller. In many cases, this continuing relationship is formalised in an explicit contract. In other cases, the contract is implicit, but it is none the less important. The contract precludes daily variation of the price to accommodate short-term fluctuations in demand and supply. That is not to deny that auction-markets do exist, but we do deny that they are the only markets that exist. Auction-markets do not provide an adequate model with which to explain macroeconomic phenomena.

The rational expectations model embodies an auction view of the labour market. It is assumed that wages adjust rapidly to equate supply and demand. All unemployment is voluntary – the unemployed are mistaken about the current market-clearing wage. Yet the long-term, contractual nature of the relationship is especially characteristic of the labour market. With some important exceptions, the employment relationship is founded on the expectation on both sides that it will persist for a substantial time. In fact, several of the terms of that contract, such as superannuation, are explicitly designed to cement a long-term relationship.

The view of the labour market which underlies the rational expectations macro models has been supported by a misinterpretation of labour market statistics on turnover. Statistics show that labour-market turnover is high and the average duration of unemployment spells is low. This is taken to imply a surprisingly fluid labour market in which people flow into and out of the unemployment pool frequently and spend only a short time unemployed. This is entirely consistent with the view that all unemployment is voluntary, and results from misperceptions regarding the 'true' wage rate.

This picture is misleading because these frequent periods of unemployment are not evenly distributed across the population. Further, many unemployment spells are ended by leaving the labour force rather than finding employment. As a result, 'most unemployment is the result of a relatively small part of the population suffering repeated, extended spells' (Clark and Summers, 1979, p. 46). The concentration of long spells of unemployment is inconsistent with the view that unemployment is an individual, optimising response to misperceptions of current reality. Rather, it is consistent with a view in which wages are sticky and labour-markets fail to clear. Various authors have studied macroeconomic models with some rigidity of prices and wages together with rational expectations (see for example Fischer, 1977; Hoel, 1979; and Phelps and Taylor, 1977).

Non-treatment of capital

At this point, we should emphasise the extremely simplistic nature of the basic impotence model. It includes no assets, no capital accumulation, no taxes, no inventories. It is a very classical model, in which there is a sharp dichotomy between real and monetary phenomena. It is a model in which money has no *real* role. Not surprisingly, the policy-impotence-result depends crucially on these simplifications. A full exposition of the results of incorporating capital accumulation, inventories and taxes into the basic impotence model would be a major undertaking. Instead, we merely sketch the main ideas.

In the basic impotence model, money is *neutral*, in the sense that a fully-anticipated change in the money supply has no *real* outcomes (it merely alters the price level). However, even if money is neutral in this sense, a fully-anticipated change in the rate of growth of money supply will alter the real interest rate, and thus have an effect on rate of capital accumulation (Tobin, 1965; Johnson, 1978b). It will therefore affect the level of output in the long run.[1] Thus, when we introduce capital into the model, monetary policy can have real effects – it is not impotent.

It seems reasonable to assume that inventory accumulation also depends upon the real interest rate, which depends upon the anticipated rate of inflation. Therefore, even fully-anticipated monetary policy will have real effects on output for inventories (Blinder and Fischer, 1981).

Finally, the tax system is clearly far from neutral. The most

---

[1]Money is said to be *superneutral* if all real variables are invariant to different rates of growth of the money supply (Buiter, 1980, p. 39). Though it is possible to construct models in which money is superneutral, they involve rather special assumptions.

obvious non-neutrality is the progressivity of the income tax. Inflation has real effects by decreasing real disposable incomes, with consequent effects on consumption, saving and investment (see for example Feldstein, Green and Sheshinski, 1978).

Persistence

Many authors have adopted a different line of attack against the rational expectations models. They have argued that they simply do not fit the facts. It is well known that unemployment is highly serially correlated – that is, if the unemployment rate is above average in any given year, it is likely to be above average again the next year. Or, to put it differently, booms and slumps tend to last more than a single year – they tend to persist. This is demonstrated in Figure 5.1, which depicts unemployment rates for the UK and US for this century.

Persistence is the Achilles heel of these models. To see this, consider again the model of Chapter 4, where the supply function is:

$$y_t = Y + \delta(p_t - p^*_t) + u_t$$
$$y_t - Y = \delta(p_t - p^*_t) + u_t$$

The dilemma is that we observe that the left-hand side of the above equation is serially correlated.[1] That implies that at least one of the terms on the right-hand side must also be serially correlated. It is a fundamental tenet of rational expectations that expectation errors are random and, in particular, are *not* serially correlated. Therefore, we cannot seek an explanation for the observed serial correlation in the first term. There only remains the error term, u_t, which represents random shifts in the supply curve. This must bear the brunt of explaining persistent deviations of unemployment from the natural rate.

Hall (1975) estimates that only 1.7 per cent of the variation in unemployment in the US from 1954 to 1974 was attributable to expectation errors. The remaining 98.3 per cent must be attributed

[1]The concept of serial correlation is discussed in the appendix to Chapter 2.

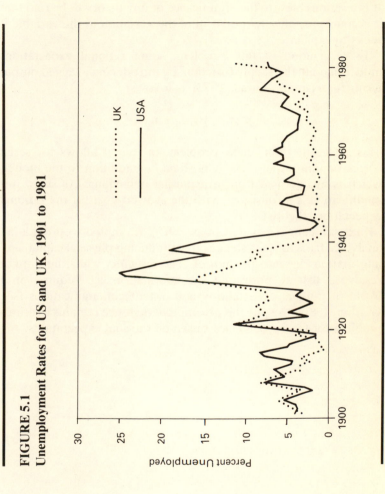

FIGURE 5.1
Unemployment Rates for US and UK, 1901 to 1981

to unexplained shifts in the supply curve. The natural rate/rational expectations model '*contains no explanation whatever of the persistence of unemployment* but merely identifies it with an unexplained shift in the ... (supply equation)' (Hall, 1975, pp. 312–13). It is a serious blow to the significance of any theory to be told that it accounts for only 1.7 per cent of the variation in the variable it seeks to explain.

In recognition of this problem, some rational expectations models modify the supply function, by introducing a lagged output term (for example, Lucas, 1973) as follows:

$$y_t = Y + \delta(p_t - p^*_t) + \beta y_{t-1} + u_t$$

This solves the immediate problem, in that it allows for serial correlation in output. Yet, it is an *ad hoc* addition to the model, which is not derived from maximising behaviour. As such, this modification is inconsistent with the avowed goals of the rational expectations theorists.

In a subsequent paper, Lucas (1975) attempted to provide an analytical basis for persistence, by introducing physical capital and information lags into the model. The difficulty which he did not resolve is that of motivating the information lags required in a world of rational expectations and instant communications (see Gordon, 1981). Despite this attempt, persistence remains a serious problem for macroeconomics based on rational expectations.

Does the World Fit the Models?

6

The theory of rational expectations poses a fundamental challenge to the established orthodoxy that governments can and should utilise a variety of demand-management policies to maintain full employment. More specifically, 'rational expectations' have been interpreted to imply that policy-makers cannot, even in the short run, alter the level of unemployment systematically through the management of aggregate demand. Clearly the implications for macroeconomic policy are enormous. But is the theory right?

We have already argued that rational expectations theory is appealing to economists since it is consistent with their general views about the way in which economic agents go about their business. The fact that the theory is intuitively appealing does little to establish its validity as a description of the world however. Doubts have been raised about the unbiasedness of rational expectations where information is costly. Moreover, there are serious misgivings about the empirical validity of the class of macroeconomic model upon which the impotence of policy result is based. Most would agree that these doubts must be resolved and the validity of the theory tested by appeal to empirical evidence. There is less agreement on how to interpret the evidence.

The theory of rational expectations and its confrontation with the data is an interesting case history in economic methodology (Maddock, 1984). The theory of knowledge – when does theory become fact? – is a problem which has troubled philosophers for centuries. A degree of consensus has been achieved, but problems remain. In economics, as in other sciences, the actual criteria employed in validating a theory are considerably less stringent than the official rhetoric would have us believe.

Economists appear to advocate two different approaches to the issue of empirical validation. One view suggests that the realism of the model and its assumptions are crucial. The other view holds that the assumptions are irrelevant to the acceptability of the theory – the only relevant criterion is how well the model predicts. In the former view, rational expectations models would have to be rejected if it was demonstrated that economic agents do not actually have unbiased expectations. In the latter view, rational expectations models would be favoured if they could predict the future better than alternative models.

However, neither of these views is an adequate description of the way in which economic research is actually conducted. Few, if any, empirical tests in economics are decisive. Different techniques generate different results. Seldom (never?) is a theory rejected on the basis of a single confrontation with the data.

Instead of determined reliance on a decisive empirical tests, arguments in economics are conducted on a variety of levels. For example, in this book we started with the proposition that rational expectations were *consistent* with the traditional economic approach to individual behaviour. We then discussed macroeconomic theory and policy, and showed that it was an *important problem* with which economic theory needed to deal. Next, we discussed the *power* of the impotence model and its potential significance for macroeconomic policy. In the previous chapter, we analysed the weaknesses of some of the *assumptions* of the theory. In this chapter, we will discuss some of the *statistical evidence* for the theory. Each of these questions is important in assessing any theory, and they will each figure, implicitly or explicity, in the progress and development of agreed knowledge.

Therefore, the statistical work arising from rational expectations should be evaluated from a perspective in which one's faith in a theory depends on a variety of considerations, of which statistical evidence is merely a part. We should not expect to find a single statistical test or result which is decisive in convincing us forever that rational expectations models are true, or persuading us that they are false. Science, especially social science, does not operate in that manner. Rather, the process is cumulative. Evidence and

arguments accumulate, and economists have to assess the conflicting results and decide ultimately whether or not rational expectations provide a more fruitful viewpoint from which to study,
document and change the world. We have to balance the statistical
evidence against considerations of logic, fruitfulness and consistency, before deciding whether to work in the rational expectations mould.

6.1 Direct Tests

The rational expectations hypothesis implies that expectations
should have certain properties. In particular, they should be
unbiased predictors of the actual values and they should be based
on all the information available at the time of their formation.
Therefore, an obvious test is to investigate whether or not
expectations in fact exhibit these properties. Unfortunately,
however, expectations are not directly observable.

There are a large number of surveys of reported expectations
covering a variety of countries, variables and time-periods. These
include, for example, consumer surveys of expected inflation,
business surveys of expected sales and investment, and surveys of
'experts' regarding inflation, GNP, unemployment and so on. The
most famous of the latter is the Livingston series. Every six months
since 1947, Joseph Livingston, a US journalist, has asked a panel
of economists to forecast a number of economic variables including the consumer price index (CPI). The forecasts were published
in his newspaper column and have formed the basis of a number of
empirical studies.[1]

Unbiasedness

From the definition of rational expectations

---

[1]A comprehensive survey of direct tests of rational expectations can be found in
Aiginger (1980). He also reports his analysis of thirty-nine expectational series
from seven different countries. Since we are as much concerned with methodology
as with the results of these tests, the Livingston series figures prominently in the
examples we discuss. The particular examples we have chosen should not be
regarded as representative.

$$p^*_t = E_{t-1}p_t$$

it follows that

$$p^*_t = p_t + u_t$$

where u_t is a random error term with

$$E[u_t] = 0$$

That is, a rational expectation must be an unbiased prediction of the relevant variable.

One simple way to test for bias is to compare long-run averages of actual and expected values for a given economic series. If the expectations are rational, then the means should not be significantly different. Unfortunately, most survey forecasts do not fare too well even on this simple criterion.

A more satisfactory test of bias is to estimate an equation of the form

$$p_t = \alpha + \beta p^*_t + u_t$$

If p^* is an unbiased estimate of p, then the estimated coefficients should be $\alpha = 0$ and $\beta = 1$.

This test was first carried out by Turnovsky (1970) using the Livingston data series. Turnovsky found that he could reject the hypothesis of $\alpha = 0$ and $\beta = 1$ for the period 1954–64, but not for the period 1962–9. Turnovsky's paper has been followed by a flood of other studies using a variety of economic series. The results are mixed, but in quite a number, the hypothesis of *unbiasedness* can be statistically rejected.

It is suggestive that in Aiginger's (1980) analysis of thirty-nine different economic series, *unbiasedness* cannot be rejected for most of the expert forecasts, but can be rejected for all the consumer surveys? This is difficult for strict rational expectations theory to explain. The rational expectations hypothesis does not suggest that experts should be more rational than non-experts – in a rational expectations world, we are all experts. Of course, this finding is not difficult to explain if we allow for the costs of information. But most macroeconomic models employing rational expectations assume away information costs.

Efficiency

Unbiasedness is not a sufficient condition for rationality. To be rational in the sense of Muth, expectations should be based on all the information available at the time at which the forecast is made. Or, in other words, it should not be possible to improve on the forecast by utilising additional information which was available at the time of the forecast. This implies that there should be *no statistical relationship* between the expectation errors and the *information set* at the time of the forecast.

To clarify this point, consider the Livingston CPI series. At the time of the forecast, past values of the CPI are certainly known and therefore belong to the information set. There should be no statistical relationship between the prediction errors of the Livingston series and lagged values of the CPI. Therefore, in the regression

$$p_t - p^*_t = \alpha_1 p_{t-1} + \alpha_2 p_{t-2} + \alpha_3 p_{t-3} + \dots + \alpha_k p_{t-k} + u_t$$

all the coefficients $\alpha_1, \alpha_2, \dots, \alpha_k$ should be zero. More precisely, we should not be able to reject the joint hypothesis

$$\alpha_1 = \alpha_2 = \dots = \alpha_k = 0$$

Equivalently, there should be no statistical relationship between current prediction errors and past prediction errors. That is, rationality implies that forecast errors must be serially uncorrelated. Aiginger (1980) found serial correlation of errors in more that 50 per cent of the series he tested. This included the Livingston series, which was the only one of the experts' series to exhibit serial correlation. McNees (1978) found some evidence of serial correlation in his study of well-known US macroeconomic forecasts.

Pearce (1979) contributes a slightly different test. Using statistical forecasting methods (the so-called Box-Jenkins approach), he develops the best possible forecasting equation for the CPI, based solely on past values of the CPI. He uses this model to forecast six and twelve months ahead. The model is then updated with a further six months data, and another pair of forecasts made. This generates a series of optimal forecasts based solely on past values of the CPI. The forecast errors of this series is then compared with the forecast errors of the Livingston series. The constructed series consistently outperforms the Livingston series in terms of forecast error. We can conclude that the Livingston panel did not efficiently use all the information available in the past history of the variable they were attempting to forecast.

We would like to emphasise Pearce's methodology. He took an information set which was clearly available to the members of the Livingston panel, processed that information using commonly accepted statistical techniques and produced an expectation series which consistently outperformed the panel of experts.

While past expectation errors clearly belong to the information set at the time the forecast is made, it is not clear what else should be considered as part of the information set. But there are some obvious candidates. It is reasonable to expect past monetary growth rates to be considered in forecasting inflation. Yet Brown and Maital (1981) find a significant statistical relationship between the Livingston CPI series and lagged money growth rates.

Conclusion

We have certainly not attempted to present a comprehensive survey of reported tests of unbiasedness and efficiency (see Aiginger, 1980). Furthermore, the criteria of unbiasedness and efficiency do not exhaust the implied statistical properties of rational expectations, which have been tested empirically. We hope that we have given the reader some insight into how we might directly test the rationality of expectations, and that we have indicated some of the findings.

Taken as a whole, the literature which attempts to test the rationality of reported expectations cannot be regarded as favourable to the rational expectations hypothesis. Even a very weak test such as unbiasedness is rejected in many series. Further, proponents of rational expectations cannot take much comfort from the demonstration of cases in which rationality cannot be rejected, since failure to reject a null hypothesis does not imply acceptance of the alternative hypothesis. However, there is another way out.

Survey data is the staple of most of the social sciences. However, the economics profession as a whole has tended to regard survey data with suspicion if not hostility. Many economists fear that reported expectations do not in fact reflect the actual behaviour of economic agents. They have a strong preference for observed behaviour as the source of economic data. 'Economists hold the strong presumption, *probably justified*, that observed behaviour generally provides a better source of explanatory hypotheses than do verbal reports.' (Mills, 1962, p.33, emphasis added). Economists who have little faith in the reliability or usefulness of reported expectations need not be unduly disturbed by the failure of reported expectations to exhibit the statistical properties of rationality. Some support for this view is provided by Pearce (1979), who finds that his constructed series of inflation expectations (already discussed) is a better explanator of interest rates than the Livingston series. One interpretation of this result is that the Livingston series does not adequately represent the expectations of those active in financial markets.

Coincidentally proponents of rational expectations tend to belong to the group who have little faith in survey data. Therefore, they have resorted to empirical tests which involve observable magnitudes only. We devote the rest of this chapter to these tests.

6.2 The Output–Inflation Trade-off

In the previous section, we noted that Turnovsky (1970) found that the Livingston series was biased for the period 1954–64, but not for the period 1962–9. This suggests that it may be unreasonable to assume that economic agents follow the same expectations-generating mechanism indefinitely. The expectations mechanism may adapt to the demands of the situation. Since processing information is costly, a simple rule may suffice when economic conditions are stable. When inflation is near zero, there is not much to be gained by having an elaborate mechanism for predicting future inflation. In inflationary times, on the other hand, a simple extrapolative rule becomes inadequate and there are gains to be made by improving the efficiency of forecasts. Therefore, expectations may exhibit rationality in some periods and not in others. The same argument can be applied to different economies at a given time. In countries where inflation is high, there are rewards for rational forecasting.

This idea was used by Lucas (1973) in a cross-country study which provides some mild support for the rationality of expectations in countries of high inflation. Lucas related the slope of the short-run supply curve to the variance of average prices in nineteen countries. He found a positive relationship. That is, in countries with relatively stable prices, the short-run supply curve was far from vertical; an increase in aggregate demand would have a large initial impact on real output. Conversely, in countries with unstable prices, the supply curve was nearly vertical. Demand increases were almost instantaneously reflected in prices, with little or no effect on real output.

One possible interpretation of these results is that people living in countries with stable inflation rates did not have to invest heavily in predicting inflation. Consequently, they could be readily fooled by demand-stimulating policies. However, where inflation was variable, there were returns to more sophisticated predictions, removing the potency of demand-stimulating policies. However, where inflation was variable, there were returns to more sophisticated predictions, removing the potency of demand-management policy. These results suggest that individuals are more rational when they need to be, which should be of some comfort to the proponents of rational expectations. However, no one would claim that this is a very powerful or discriminating test of the rationality of expectations.

In addition to its intrinsic interest, we have presented the Lucas test because it clearly illustrates a problem which bedevils most indirect tests of rational expectations. The hypothesis which Lucas tests is really a joint hypothesis of the natural rate hypothesis coupled with rational expectations. By definition, an indirect test attempts to assess the rationality of expectations through the impact of expectations on observable economic variables. It requires *a priori* from the empiricist a specification of the manner in which expectations influence the observable economic variables. The results of the test will either support or contradict the joint hypotheses of rational expectations and the particular economic model. If the joint hypotheses are refuted, it is impossible to determine whether it is the hypothesis of rationality, or the economic model, or perhaps both, which should be rejected. Only recently have tools been developed which allow use of the information contained in the two theoretical propositions (that expectations are rational and that the economy is characterised by a natural rate of unemployment) but which do not integrate the two hypotheses so closely that we cannot determine which hypothesis has failed in a joint test. We will discuss these developments later in the chapter.

6.3   Testing the Natural Rate Hypothesis

In the previous chapter, we emphasised the important role which the natural rate hypothesis plays in macroeconomic models employing rational expectations. We recall that the *natural rate hypothesis* is simply the hypothesis that output (or employment) will depart from its natural level only because of expectational errors. Systematic deviations of output from its natural rate therefore require systematic expectational errors. It is typically the natural rate hypothesis which is *joined* to the assumption of rational expectations in indirect empirical tests of the latter. Can the validity of the natural rate hypothesis be independently established? In the same way as the rationality of expectations was tested separately, can we test the natural rate hypothesis alone?

Not surprisingly, such a study was attempted by a number of authors soon after Friedman postulated the natural rate hypothesis in 1968. Typically, these researchers estimated an equation of the form:

$$p_t = \alpha (u_t - u_N) + \beta p^*_t + v_t \qquad (6.1)$$

where

u_N = the natural rate of unemployment

p^*_t = expected inflation

The size of the coefficient β is crucial. The natural rate hypothesis implies that $\beta = 1$. If the estimated β is significantly less than one, the natural rate hypothesis can be rejected.

Results were as usual mixed. However, over time the coefficient β appeared to increase with inflation. That is, as this equation was estimated on later data sets, the size of the estimated coefficient approached the value of 1 (Gordon, 1976, p. 193). The early results were used to argue that the natural rate hypothesis had no empirical support. But by the mid-1970s it was grudgingly accepted that natural rate hypothesis could not be consistently rejected by the data.

There is a much more devastating critique of these results as a test of the natural rate hypothesis. The test itself is biased *against* the natural rate hypothesis. β is the coefficient on price expectations. Expectations, however, are unobservable. They must be expressed in terms of observable variables. If this representation is inappropriate, it will tend to bias the estimated size of the coefficient β downwards.[1] Many of the studies in question employed some form of distributed lag of past inflation as the proxy for expected inflation, for example:

$$p^*_t = \sum_{k=1}^{m} w_k \, p_{t-k}$$

In fact, we have returned to the dilemma we set out to avoid. We would like to be able to test the validity of the natural rate hypothesis independently of any assumption regarding the expectation of prices. In order to test the natural rate hypothesis, we need to postulate an expression of expected prices in terms of observable variables. In other words, we have to make an assumption about the formation of expectations. The jointness of the two hypotheses – rational expectations and the natural rate hypothesis seems to be unavoidable.

This may seem a trifle confusing. Economists were able to conduct tests of the rationality of expectations without making assumptions about the nature of the economy. Yet we claim that to test the natural rate hypothesis, some assumption needs to be made concerning the formation of expectations. The reason for this

---

[1] The natural rate of unemployment, u_N, is also unobservable, which provides another problem for these tests. One common solution is to assume that u_N is constant.

distinction is simply that the natural rate hypothesis is essentially an hypothesis about the use of expectations. Recall that the natural rate hypothesis suggests that output (or employment) will only depart from its natural level if expectations are wrong. Obviously, some assumption regarding expectations is necessary to test this hypothesis. On the other hand, the proposition that price expectations are rational implies that they must satisfy certain properties such as unbiasedness and efficiency. Testing for these properties does not require any assumptions about the structure of the economy.

As we have seen, direct tests of the reported expectations have been less than persuasive. However, the natural rate hypothesis applies to the aggregate economy. Demonstrating that the reported expectations for some group or other are not rational does not prove that expectations in some properly aggregated sense might not be rational. For this and perhaps other reasons, economists who believed that the economy was characterised by rational expectations proceeded to develop a series of tests of the joint hypothesis.

6.4 Testing the Combined Hypotheses

Recall equation (6.1) above:

$$p_t = \alpha(u_t - u_N) + \beta p^*_t + v_t$$

Since under the natural rate hypothesis $\beta = 1$, this can be written

$$u_t - u_{Nt} = (p_t - p^*_t)/\alpha + \epsilon_t$$

This formulation makes explicit the implications of the natural rate hypothesis; namely, that unemployment cannot depart systematically from its natural rate unless there are systematic expectational errors.

Further, assume that the natural rate of unemployment can be represented as a distributed lag of its own past values, that is:

$$u_{Nt} = \sum_{k=1}^{m} \gamma_k u_{t-k}$$

The previous equation can then be written

$$u_t = (p_t - p^*_t)/\alpha + \sum_{k=1}^{m} \gamma_k u_{t-k} + e_t$$

The hypothesis of rational expectations implies that

$$p^*_t = E[p_t : I_{t-1}]$$

or

$$E[p_t - p^*_t : I_{t-1}] = 0$$

This in turn implies that

$$E[u_t] = \sum_{k=1}^{m} \gamma_k u_{t-k}$$

Given that deviations of unemployment from its natural rate are entirely due to expectational errors, other information which was available at the time that price expectations were formed should be of no additional benefit in explaining unemployment. That is, if (x_t) is another economic series, it should have no explanatory power in the regression:

$$u_t = \sum_{k=1}^{m} \gamma_k u_{t-k} + \sum_{k=1}^{m} \eta_k x_{t-k} + \epsilon_t$$

where ϵ is a random error term. In other words, if expectations are rational and (x_t) is in the information set I_{t-1}, the coefficients η_k should not be significantly different from zero. Conversely, if one or more η_ks were not equal to zero, then some information which actually influenced unemployment *had been ignored* in the formation of expectations.

A specific example might help to clarify this test. Most macroeconomists would agree that there is an observable relationship between the price level and the recent history of the money supply. If price expectations are rational *and* if information about past money supply is available, then rational price expectations should incorporate this knowledge. Therefore, in the regression

$$u_t = \sum_{k=1}^{m} \gamma_k u_{t-k} + \eta_1 M_{t-1} + \eta_2 M_{t-2} + \eta_3 M_{t-3} + \epsilon_t$$

where M_{t-1}, M_{t-2}, M_{t-3} are lagged values of the money supply, the coefficients η_1, η_2, η_3 should not be significantly different from zero. Should this not be the case, there are two possible interpretations:

● price expectations are not rational, that is p^*_t does not equal $E[p_t]$

● the natural rate hypothesis (as we have defined it) does not hold. For example, if η_1 is not equal to 0, it might be that the correct model of the economy is

$$u_t - u_{Nt} = \alpha(p_t - p^*_t) + \eta_1 M_{t-1} + \epsilon_t$$

It should be clear that, in the event that a test of this type gives negative results, we are unable to say which of the two hypotheses is responsible. Nevertheless, if we find coefficients on other explanatory variables which are significantly different from zero, we should conclude that at least one of the two hypotheses is invalid.

Sargent (1973, 1976a) has conducted tests of this sort and found that he had to reject the null hypothesis in several equations. If one adhered to a strict programme of falsification, then one would be forced to conclude that the natural rate – rational expectations hypothesis had been rejected by the data. Instead, Sargent (1973) writes 'I imagine that the evidence would not be sufficiently compelling to persuade someone to abandon a *strongly held prior belief* in the natural rate hypothesis' (Sargent,1973, p. 462, emphasis added). In one of the more memorable phrases of empirical economics, he states that the joint hypothesis 'is not obscenely at variance with the data' (Sargent, 1976a, p. 233).

6.5 Response to Failure

The failure of his experiments to support his convictions did not lead Sargent to abandon the theory as Popperian falsification methodology would demand.* Instead, despite the setbacks, Sargent continued to work on rational expectations models and attempted to devise tests which would confirm his strongly-held

[1]Sir Karl Popper (1959) and (1962) argues that the essence of scientific research is attempts to falsify specific hypotheses. In principle falsified hypotheses should be discarded. In practice he accepts that scientists should not be quite so ready to throw away theories but they should struggle to ensure that falsification is substantial. This weakening of the rule of falsification has led to 'sophisticated falsification' and similar methodological views which are discussed in Lakatos (1970) and other sources.

prior beliefs. From the results which had been obtained so far it was clear that past information was in some way able to influence current economic variables. How was this possible if people used information efficiently in the formation of price expectations?

Similarly, how was it possible for unemployment to persist above or below the natural rate for extended periods of time? During the Great Depression unemployment persisted above its natural rate for a long time. This suggested that the effects of some event which occurred years earlier persisted through the 1930s. While the first response of rational expectations theorists to the problem of persistence was dismissive, the failure of the early tests through persistence-type effects led them to modify the theory so as to take them into account.

The most notable change involved the definition of the natural rate hypothesis. In 1972 Lucas wrote 'Let us define the natural rate hypothesis as the hypothesis that different time-paths of the general price level will be associated with time-paths of real output that do not differ *on average*' (Lucas, 1972, p. 50; emphasis in the original). The natural rate hypothesis then specified a degree of independence of output (or unemployment) levels and prices. This independence was incorporated into a simple aggregate macroeconomic model and tested together with the assumption of rational expectations. As we have seen the tests failed. Sargent explains:

> The natural rate hypothesis is taken to assert that only the *currently* unexpected part of inflation (or of any other variable) affects unemployment. Neither the expected part of inflation nor any lagged unexpected rate of inflation is permitted to affect unemployment. Now this seems to be a much too stringent interpretation of the natural rate hypothesis, in the sense that one can produce a model which would deliver all the 'neutrality' results associated with the natural rate hypothesis but which at the same time is rejected by the tests ... Such models are arrived at by considering the implication of permitting *lagged* unexpected parts of inflation (or any other variable) to affect unemployment.
>
> (Sargent, 1976b, p. 73; emphasis in original)

The natural rate hypothesis was thus refined to suit this new conviction developed out of the failure of the empirical tests. Sargent seems concerned to focus on the neutrality of policy proposition, suggesting that that is the important component of the theoretical framework which has to be retained in any revised formulation of the natural rate hypothesis.

The models we have considered so far allow only the *current* expectation errors to influence the deviation of output from its natural rate. Sargent suggests that there are a number of possible mechanisms for price expectations to influence unemployment – current expected prices, current unexpected price shocks, past expected prices and past unexpected price shocks. The version of the natural rate hypothesis that he then goes on to favour is that no expected prices can have any influence on deviations of unemployment from the natural rate but that both current and past shocks can have an effect. If price expectations were badly wrong in 1929 this might have had an influence which continued through much of the decade of the 1930s. This theoretical modification offers an explanation of the persistence phenomenon. It could also explain why the statistical tests found that past information about other variables (for example the money supply) influenced the current deviation of unemployment from the natural rate, since past price errors may be correlated with these other variables.

Lucas constructed a theoretical model in which persistence could be explained yet which retained the neutrality of policy, which is the main emphasis of this and related models. Past forecast errors have effects which persist because economic agents are restricted in their information so that they do not know precisely the magnitude of their expectational errors and hence they cannot correct the errors. In Lucas's model, this is achieved by locating people on 'islands' where they have local information but no aggregate information to infer aggregate economic conditions. They make investment decisions on the basis of what they infer about aggregate economic decisions. Inevitably, forecast errors are made in the investment decisions and the effects of these persist into the future. In this way, business cycles are generated.

The government's problem in this model is to devise a policy rule to stabilise the economy. The solution depends upon what is assumed about the government's information. One can assume either that this is restricted to the same information as other agents or that the government has superior information. If the government has the same information as other agents and private expectations of government action are formed rationally, then the *unexpected* component of price changes is independent of the *systematic* part of government policy. If current and past unexpected price shocks alone can influence the deviation of output from its natural rate and no systematic policy rule can influence price shocks, policy remains impotent. On the other hand, if the government has better information than the public, it can design a policy rule which will exploit this informational advantage and help stabilise the economy. The government could, however, achieve the same degree of stabilisation simply by passing on its superior information to all other agents. Sargent and Wallace (1975) trace out these implications of rational expectations at a less technical level than Lucas (1972).

It is clear that these developments, which arose out of the failure of the tests and the need to allow for the persistence of deviations from the natural rate, changed the focus of the search for empirical support for the rational expectations hypothesis. No longer was the emphasis on tests of the *natural rate hypothesis*; it was switched to the *impotence of policy*.

6.6   Only Unanticipated Policy Matters

So far, we have considered tests of rational expectations itself, the natural rate hypothesis and rational expectations and natural rate combined. With the failure of the earlier tests, rational expectations theorists weakened their maintained hypothesis slightly and sought support for the proposition that government policy is impotent if expectations are rational. The essence of this proposition is that only unanticipated policy can affect the level of unemployment. But of course unanticipated policy can reflect past as well as current errors of policy forecasting. The history of attempts to test for the impotence of policy illustrates yet again the pitfalls of empirical economic research.

In Chapter 4, we derived the following equation for the level of output:

$$y_t - Y = \frac{\alpha\delta(x_t - Ex_t) - \beta u_t}{\beta + \delta}$$

which can be expressed more simply as:

$$y_t - Y = h(x_t - Ex_t) - w_t$$

where

$$h = \alpha\delta/(\beta + \delta)$$

and

$$w_t = \beta u_t/(\beta + \delta)$$

This equation states that the level of output will deviate from its natural level only to the extent that policy (represented by x_t) is unanticipated or because of the random factor u_t. We then went on to argue that, under rational expectations, systematic policy will be fully anticipated and therefore ineffective in changing the level of output. This is the impotence of policy result in its strongest form. The modification which was made to the research programme after the criticism of persistence and the failure of the earlier statistical tests can be represented as follows:

$$y_t - Y = h_1 (x_t - Ex_t) + h_2 (x_{t-1} - Ex_{t-1}) + \dots + w_t$$

where the h_ts are constants and w_t is a random disturbance. The deviation of output from its natural rate is thus a consequence of the error made in forecasting policy in the current period ($x_t - Ex_t$) the error made in forecasting policy in the preceding period ($x_{t-1} - Ex_{t-1}$) and so on, plus a current random disturbance (w_t).

If we could divide policy into its anticipated and unanticipated components, we could directly test this result. The problem was of course to estimate the policy rule accurately. Barro (1977) pioneered such a test. He based it precisely on separating out the effects of anticipated and unanticipated money growth.

In the theoretical model developed in Chapter 4, the policy variable x_t can be any policy tool capable of shifting the aggregate demand curve. Tests of policy rules in the rational expectations literature have concentrated exclusively on monetary policy. Since tax rates and other fiscal policy tools almost invariably have an effect on labour (and other) supply decisions, it is simpler to focus on monetary policy. However, it is important to realise that if the results demonstrate that monetary policy is impotent, we cannot infer that fiscal policy is similarly ineffective. More fundamentally, is it valid to assume that monetary policy works solely through the demand side and has no effect on supply decisions? This assumption has been criticised by Tobin (see his comments on Sargent, 1973), who argues that it is too restrictive to assume that changes in the supply of a financial asset (money) will have no influence on the supply of other goods and services. Despite these criticisms, the empirical tests proceeded under the assumption that the relevant policy variable was the money supply.

Barro first estimated the equation

$$m_t = \alpha + \beta_1 m_{t-1} + \beta_2 m_{t-2} + \gamma g_t + \delta u_{t-1} + \epsilon_t$$

where

m_t = money growth rate
g_t = growth rate of real government expenditure
u_t = unemployment rate (as a proxy for $Y_t - Y$)
ϵ_t = random error term

This equation was then used to divide the money growth series into anticipated (m^*_t) and unanticipated ($m_t - m^*_t$) components. The predicted values of this equation (m^*_t) were regarded as the anticipated component, and the residuals (the differences between the actual and predicted values) as the unanticipated component.

According to the impotence result, only the unanticipated component (the residuals from the above equation) should be able to explain deviations of output or employment from its natural rate. Barro tested this by estimating an equation of the form:

$$Y_t - Y = \alpha_0(m_t - m^*_t) + \alpha_1(m_{t-1} - m^*_{t-1})$$
$$+ \alpha_2(m_{t-2} - m^*_{t-2}) + b_0 m^*_t + b_1 m^*_{t-1} + b_2 m^*_{t-2} + e_t$$

where $\{(m - m^*)_t\}$ are the residuals from the previous equation. This form allowed both the unanticipated and anticipated components of monetary policy to influence the deviation of y_t from Y. ($m_t - m^*_t$) corresponds to $x_t - Ex_t$ in equation (6.2). His hypothesis that the inclusion of the anticipated components $\{m^*_t\}$ did not contribute to the explanatory power of the equation was confirmed by his results. The terms $\{(m_t - m^*)\}$ were significant explanatory variables in the equation while as a group the $\{m^*\}$ terms were not. The unanticipated component of the money supply affected unemployment while the anticipated component did not. Monetary policy was impotent.

Barro's results provided the strongest support thus far obtained for the impotence result, but they did not long remain unchallenged. Arguing that there were statistical flaws in Barro's technique, Mishkin (1982) produced a variation of the Barro test which soundly rejects the 'only unanticipated policy matters' conclusion.[1]

Mishkin proposed a method of testing which not only allowed an assessment of the validity of the joint hypothesis but also of each hypothesis separately. To do this he used a statistical technique which allows one to judge which of a pair of competing models best explains a set of data by comparing the residuals derived from estimating the competing models. Mishkin developed four related models:

- with rationality of expectations and policy neutrality
- with rationality of expectations alone
- with neutrality of policy alone
- an unrestricted model

By comparing the models pair by pair, Mishkin was able to rank the empirical support for each model. On the basis of these tests, he strongly rejected the joint hypothesis relative to the unrestricted model, found little support for that based on neutrality alone and some support for the model based on rational expectations alone. Even more damning for the neutrality hypothesis was that he found that anticipated policy was always more potent and more significant than unanticipated policy, which is a direct contradiction of the neutrality hypothesis.

Mishkin's tests used a version of the aggregate supply curve which distinguished separately the effects of anticipated policy from these of unanticipated policy in the same way as Barro had proposed:

$$
\begin{aligned}
y_t - Y = {} & \alpha_0 \, (m_t - m^*_t) + \alpha_1 \, (m_{t-1} - m^*_{t-1}) \\
& + \alpha_2 \, (m_{t-2} - m^*_{t-2}) + \\
& + \beta_0 m^*_t + \beta_1 m^*_{t-1} + \beta_2 m^*_{t-2} + \epsilon_t
\end{aligned}
$$

[1] We should mention that Mishkin was not the first to criticise Barro's results; see, for example, Small (1979). Further, Barro has extended and developed his test in subsequent publications – Barro (1979), Barro and Rush (1980) – and received additional support from Leiderman (1980).

the test of neutrality was the same as Barro, namely the hypothesis:

$$\beta_0 = \beta_1 = \beta_2 = \dots 0$$

Mishkin's tests differed in that he allowed for the possibility that the expectation of policy variable m^*_t may not have been formed rationally. Where Barro insisted that the constructed term m^*_t in the test equation was the best that could be found on the basis of the evidence from an equation like:

$$m^*_t = \gamma + \delta Z_{t-1} + v_t \qquad \text{(Barro)}$$

Mishkin allowed for the possibility that the m^*_t had been formed on the basis of the data in Z_{t-1} but with different parameters, say

$$m^*_t = \gamma' + \delta' Z_{t-1} + v_t \qquad \text{(Mishkin)} \qquad (6.3)$$

For expositional ease we will simplify the supply equation to

$$y_t - Y = \alpha(m_t - m^*_t) + \beta m^*_t + \epsilon_t \qquad (6.4)$$

Mishkin actually estimated the equation:

$$y_t - Y = \alpha(m_t - \gamma' - \delta' Z^*_{t-1}) + \beta\gamma' + \beta\delta' Z_{t-1} + \epsilon_t \qquad (6.5)$$

together with the policy rule equation (6.3) and a variety of restrictions. The most restricted model was one in which:

$$\beta = 0 \qquad \text{(imposing neutrality)} \qquad (6.6)$$

and

$$\gamma' = \gamma, \delta' = \delta \qquad \text{(imposing rationality)} \qquad (6.7)$$

Equation (6.6) requires that policy be impotent and equation (6.7) that the actual expectations of policy used be the same as the rational expectation. Thus the group of equations (6.3), (6.5), (6.6) and (6.7) comprise the full rational expectations/neutrality model. He then estimated (6.3), (6.5) and (6.6) relaxing the rationality restriction but maintaining neutrality; equations (6.3), (6.5), and (6.7) relaxing neutrality while maintaining rationality (this model is the same as Barro); and finally equations (6.3) and (6.5) with no restrictions of rationality or neutrality. This sequential method allowed Mishkin to assess which model described the data best. As cited above, the results were strongly unfavourable to the neutrality proposition and produced little support for rationality.

A closer analysis of Mishkin's results reveals that the main factor which contributed to sharp differences between his results and those of Barro involved the length of the lags represented in the estimated equations. In estimating the policy rule equation, Mishkin allowed lags of twenty quarters whereas Barro allowed only seven quarters. Indeed, when Mishkin estimated his model with truncated (seven quarter) lags, he obtained very similar results to Barro. This suggests that the question of why the effects of policy changes between two and five years earlier should still influence output in expectations-based macro models requires further research. The other question which is highlighted by these results concerns the adequacy of the supply equation as a reduced form. Perhaps an alternative model specification would receive better support from the data.

6.7 Conclusion

Our discussion of the role of testing in the development of rational expectations has revealed the existence of two quite different approaches to testing – direct tests and those incorporating macro models. The direct tests based on samples of reported forecasts of future prices have generally not supported the proposition that expectations are formed rationally. By and large reported expectations are either biased or inefficient or perhaps both. Economists tend to be suspicious of such tests on two grounds. First, it is not clear that people report their actual expectations, or more precisely, that their reported expectations are identical to the expectations on which they base market decisions. Second, the impotence of policy proposition is based solely on the requirement that in some aggregate sense expectations are unbiased. Even if expectations are inefficient and vary greatly around the true value, there is no basis for effective policy unless the errors are systematic, that is the expectations are biased. Demonstrating that surveyed expectations are inefficient may imply that people do not use all the information available and hence do not really form their expectations rationally, but that irrationality may not provide any leverage for policy. Further, even if surveyed expectations are biased, that does not mean that aggregate expectations as represented in a macroeconomic model are biased. In surveys all respondents are usually given equal weight in determining the aggregate, whereas in the economy the expectations of some agents are more important than others. It is possible to believe that survey expectations are biased but that expectations in the aggregate are not.

Despite the poor results obtained from survey evidence and the obvious appeal of such a simple test, these results have had little influence on the development of rational expectations models. Many theorists seem to act as if this type of evidence were invalid. While they may be able to explain it at some future date they choose to ignore it at the moment and to proceed as if it did not exist.

At first, such an attitude might appear unscientific and perhaps even dishonest, but this is not really the case. When Newton first articulated his gravitational theory he was challenged on every side and counter-evidence of every type was presented. Gradually over the course of a century these anomalies in the initial theory were integrated into the explanatory framework. Newton was clearly aware of many of these problems but he refused to be distracted from the main thrust of his work. He did not ignore the data in general, but he had clearly decided which types of evidence would cause him to modify his theory and which could for the time being be ignored (see Lakatos, 1970, especially pp. 133–6). Rational expectations theorists have apparently decided that the development of their theoretical apparatus will not be distracted at this stage by survey evidence on expectations.

Rational expectations theorists were concerned with evidence and with testing, but only when it was derived from within suitable macroeconomic models. The first round of such tests assumed that no past information, information which had been available when price forecasts were formed, could have any influence on deviations of unemployment from the natural rate. Such models performed badly. It was clear that fluctuations in unemployment were influenced by past economic events. The nature of this failure was closely related to some of the criticism which had been made of the models. It had been pointed out that economic time series are characterised by long swings; periods of below normal economic activity tend to persist as do periods of boom. The effects of past shocks persist. While this criticism had been ignored by rational expectations theorists when posed in isolation, its cogency was brought home by the failure of their statistical tests.

Reformulating the models as a result of these failures, rational expectations theorists again tried to find empirical support for their propositions. The new models focused upon the distinction between anticipated and unanticipated policy. Barro split monetary policy into these two components assuming that expectations were rational. He found that, while the past and currently unanticipated components of monetary policy had some effect on employment and output, the anticipated component had no effect. Though it was challenged for a variety of reasons, this result provided the most convincing evidence then available in support of rational expectations macro models.

As so often happens in economics, this result was subsequently overturned. Mishkin developed a model and testing procedure which allowed him to test for the rationality of expectations and for the neutrality of policy jointly *or* separately within the same framework. He also used a somewhat sounder statistical procedure for conducting the tests. He was able to duplicate Barro's results in support of the joint hypothesis of neutrality and rationality when (as had Barro) he restricted the lags to less than two years. But when he extended the lags up to five years, these results were contradicted. He found no evidence in support of policy neutrality – in fact, anticipated policy was more effective than unanticipated policy. Rational expectations received somewhat more support from these tests, but still did not perform convincingly.

Looking Backward and Looking Forward 7

Most of the story of this book has been written as if there were just two competing visions of the macroeconomy giving rise to just two ongoing programmes of research interacting with one another. Clearly this is an over-simplification. There are other programmes of research. Despite this it has become customary to explain the evoultion of macroeconomic thought in the 1950s and 1960s as one of conflict between monetarists and Keynesians and important aspects of this division have carried over to the separation of theorists in the 1970s and 1980s into policy passivists and policy activists. Whereas monetarists had argued that monetary policy was more efective than fiscal policy in managing the aggregate levels of demand in an economy, the policy passivists have gone a step further in their insistence that policy is impotent.

When Milton Friedman outlined his 'Theoretical Framework for Monetary Analysis' in 1970 he insisted that 'one purpose of setting forth this framework is to document my belief that the basic differences among economists are empirical, not theoretical' (Gordon, 1974, p.61). In response to this paper James Tobin was more pessimistic about resolving the differences between economists empirically 'if the monetarists and the neo-Keynesians could agree as to which values of which parameters in which behaviour relations imply which policy conclusions, then they could concentrate on the evidence regarding the values of those parameters. I

144

wish that this contribution (of Friedman's) had brought us closer to this goal but I'm afraid it has not (Gordon, 1974, p.77). Paul Davidson also responded to Friedman's essay by pointing out the conceptual rather than empirical differences between Keynes and Friedman which he felt 'do add up to a fundamentally different paradigm involving significantly different conclusions' (Gordon, 1974, p. 107). Interestingly, Davidson berated Friedman for his failure to include uncertainty in his theoretical framework. Thus it seems that while Friedman felt that the differences between his views and those of his critics could be reconciled by an appeal to evidence, at least two of his critics felt that was not the case.

Are the debates between competing groups of economists such that they can be solved by data? It seems not. Economic models are usually composed of just a few equations, yet the world as we know it is exceedingly complex and also evolving. To test theories one needs to translate concepts into variables, to develop statistics which approximate these variables, and to find econometric and other statistical techniques which allow one to distinguish between different theoretical predictions. If a prediction of the theory fails some empirical test theorists can easily redefine the variables, the statistics or the testing method in an attempt to overcome the failure. In the rational expectations programmme we saw that the failure of the information-based first round of tests led to a change in the definition of the *natural rate hypothesis* to reduce it to the *impotence of anticipated policy hypothesis*. Later Barro's results demonstrating the ineffectiveness of anticipated monetary policy on employment were challenged by Small (1979). The criticism in part was based on the belief that Barro had not correctly adjusted his labour-force data to deal with the disruptions of World War Two and the Vietnam War. Barro (1979) responded by showing that his main results were not disturbed by a more adequate treatment of the labour force. These are two examples of the way in which a large variety of elements which are interposed between a theoretical concept and an actual test can be adjusted in defence of one's concept when a contrary empirical example is found. A number of similar adjustments were made in the dispute between monetarists and neo-Keynesians, as is documented in Blaug (1980). It does seem clear that, contrary to Friedman's assertion, disputes between groups of economists are not easily resolved. The distance between an economic vision and any test of it is so large as inevitably to allow for adjustments which can deflect the point of criticism.

If we accept this as inevitable two questions seem to arise: (i) just what is the role of data and testing in the development of research programmes in economics, and (ii) what function is served by conflict between programmes if disputes are unlikely to be settled? The heavy emphasis placed by economists on econometrics and testing suggests that it is important. One of the major differences between contemporary economic training and that of earlier periods seems to lie in the heavy emphasis now placed on more sophisticated econometric analysis. If these additional skills do not allow one easily to distinguish the merits of competing theories, what function do they serve?

Clearly one goal is to allow economists to give quantitative advice on policy. Having estimated a model of the economy, it is possible to predict that an x per cent increase in the money supply will produce a y per cent increase in the rate of inflation. However, such predictions are conditional upon the accuracy of the model. If the economist believes in the model, then he or she will believe that the predicted y per cent increase will actually occur. Research of this sort can be very valuable and has been classified as 'normal science' by Thomas Kuhn (1970). The scientist involved is not attempting to develop theory but rather to apply it.

On the other hand it is clear that Sargent and Barro in their empirical work which we discussed in the previous chapter had a different objective. They were trying to advance our knowledge of the nature of the economy. They felt that it was necessary to demonstrate that their models fitted data better than some alternatives. When tests proved unconvincing, they modified concepts within their models or refined their test procedures and data in an endeavour to discover more about the nature of the economy. The discussion in Chapter 6 should be taken as an illustration of the way in which economists working within a research programme whose frontiers they are attempting to expand use data to guide their research. Empirical information plays an important role in stimulating development *within* economic research programmes even if it is unlikely to enable us to choose *between* programmes.

If data and evidence contribute mainly to research within a programme or vision, what function is served by conflict between visions? In some cases it seems little is achieved. The major Marxist visions of the economy seem to provide little stimulus or challenge to the mainstream programmes we have considered in this work, though one might argue that the orientation of Keynesian research towards the elimination of mass unemployment was stimulated by Marxist analyses of the nature of capitalist economies during the Great Depression. While there seems to be little contemporary contact between these visions now, there is certainly a regular interchange between rational expectations theorists and interventionist-oriented macroeconomists. Although we have cited the debate between Friedman and his critics in *Milton Friedman's Monetary Framework: A Debate with his Critics* (Gordon, 1974) as just one forum of macroeconomic intercourse, the journals have been peppered with thrust and counterthrust by proponents of the different visions. Much of this has taken place in three leading economics journals: the *American Economic Review*, the *Economic Journal* and the *Journal of Political Economy*, but it has carried over to virtually all journals which publish macroeconomic research. Fortunately the protagonists share a common vocabulary, and a similar set of tools of analysis, allowing for a sustantial discourse.

The earlier chapters have traced out the main developments of the rational expectations programme. In the next section of this chapter we break with this approach and focus upon the contributions made to the macroeconomics of those who favour activist policy as a consequence of the challenges thrown up by rational expectations macrotheory. These are the intellectual legacies already apparent from the interactions of research programmes. We shall see that the conflict has been fruitful. The subsequent section tries to assess the present state of the rational expectations macroeconomic research programme. Battered by critics, but clearly stimulated by its own sense of purpose, what has it achieved?

7.1 How has Economics Changed?

Rational expectations macrotheory has thrown out three main challenges to the competing activist research programme. First

and most obvious is the assertion that policy is impotent: 'An
accurate understanding of how expectations are formed leads to
the conclusion that short-run macroeconomic stabilisation policies
are untenable ... The Federal Reserve and the Treasury should
concentrate their attention on the prevention or reduction (if such
is desired) of inflation not of unemployment' (McCallum, 1980,
pp. 37 and 43). At this level of generality, their argument has had
some sway and, as we argued in Chapter 1, seemed particularly
persuasive in the political and intellectral milieu of the period.
Nevertheless ideas about the possible impotence of policy had
been around for a long time and, for theorists who were dubious
about the proposition, a new 'proof' of impotence was hardly
likely to prove convincing without considerable further evidence.

Second, the rational expectations programme has had a major
influence on the way in which expectations are treated in
economics. Older, more *ad hoc*, methods for introducing expectations into models are suspect and the idea that the expectations of
a variable should normally be considered as the unbiased estimate
of that variable has come to be widely accepted.

Although the implications of rational expectations for the
treatment of expectations have produced a significant change in
economic practice, this has been overshadowed by the third main
challenge of rational expectations – namely, that changes in policy
produce changes in expectations. To understand this we can go
back to a simple model of the macroeconomy:

$$y_t = Y + \delta p_t - \delta' p^*_t + u_t \tag{7.1}$$

$$y_t = \alpha x_t - \beta p_t + w_t \tag{7.2}$$

where equation (7.1) is a simple aggregate supply curve and
equation (7.2) an aggregate demand curve in which the government controls the policy variable x_t. The problem faced by the
policy-maker is at what level to set the policy variable to achieve a
particular target level of income. The reduced form equation for
income is:

$$y_t = \frac{\beta Y - \beta\delta' p^*_t + \alpha\delta x_t + \beta u_t + \delta w_t}{\beta + \delta} \tag{7.3}$$

If one desires to achieve a level of income of y_0, the level of the instrument x_t has to be chosen so that:

$$x_t = \frac{(\beta + \delta)\, y_0 - \beta Y + \beta\delta' p^*_t - \beta u_t - \delta w_t}{\alpha\delta}$$

or assuming u_t, w_t are zero

$$x_t = \frac{(\beta + \delta)\, y_0 - \beta Y + \beta\delta' p^*_t}{\alpha\delta} \tag{7.4}$$

The problem for the policy maker is that p^*_t, the public expectations of prices in period t, is generally unknown. When economists thought that the best assumption to make about price expectations was that they were a simple weighted average of past prices such as

$$p^*_t = \sum_{k=1}^{n} w_{k-1} p_{t-k}$$

the level for the policy variable became

$$x_t = \frac{(\beta + \delta)\, y_0 - \beta Y + \beta\delta \sum_{k=1}^{n} w_{k-1} p_{t-k} \alpha\delta}{\alpha\delta} \tag{7.5}$$

By choosing the level of x_t given by equation (7.5) policy-makers believed that they could cause the economy to shift to a level of output y_0.

The problem with the analysis was forcefully pointed out by Lucas. Considering the structural equations (7.1) and (7.2) he focussed attention on the reduced-form equation for prices which parallels the equation for income:

$$p_t = \frac{\delta' p^*_1 + \alpha x_t - Y + w_t - u_t}{\beta + \delta} \tag{7.6}$$

This reflects the well-known proposition that a policy stimulus x_t was likely to influence the price level. But if a change in policy caused a change in prices, surely it was unreasonable to expect that price expectations would follow a process like:

$$p^*_t = \sum_{k=1}^{n} w_{k-1} p_{t-k}$$

More precisely, Lucas argued that the policy-maker simply *could not assume* that the process-generating price expectations were invariant to the policy chosen. Yet some estimate of the price expectation p_t^* is necessary in order to calculate the level of x_t required to produce a target level of income as can be seen from equation (7.4):

$$x_t = \frac{(\beta + \delta) \, y_0 - \beta Y + \beta \delta' p^*_t}{\alpha \delta}$$

One cannot calculate the desired level of x_t simply from a knowledge of the desired target y_0. Yet p_t^* depends on x_t, so we need some way of discovering the relationship between these two before we can calculate the desired policy level.

Much policy advice in the 1960s and early 1970s was based on models like that given by equations (7.1) and (7.2), with specific recommendations derived from equations such as (7.4). Price expectations were then taken to have been formed as weighted averages of past prices, producing preferred policy levels such as that given in (7.5). Rational expectations theorists insisted that this approach was wrong. Since it was clear that the levels set for policy variables influenced prices, they argued that *price expectations would change as policies changed*. One could not assume that expectations were based on simple averages of past prices if one was going to alter policy levels.

The logic of the rational expectations approach in the context of our model required that expectations be derived from equation (7.6):

$$E[p_t] = \frac{E[\delta' p^*_t] + E[\alpha x_t] - E[Y] + E[w_t - u_t]}{\beta + \delta}$$

$$= \frac{\delta' p^*_t + \alpha E[x_t] - Y}{\beta + \delta}$$

or

$$p^*_t = \frac{\alpha E[x_t] - Y}{\beta + \delta - \delta'}$$

which makes quite explicit the connection between price expectations and policy. Imposing the restriction $\delta' = \delta$ on the aggregate supply equation leads directly to the impotence of policy result derived in Chapter 4.

It should be clear from our earlier discussion that any model of the type used here (equations (7.1) and (7.2) will produce non-neutral results if δ' is not equal to δ. Though the impotence result is crucially dependent on the specific form of the models used, the challenge to policy activism does not depend on a specific model. It is considerably more general. In virtually any model of the economy, the price level will depend on policy variables. If the expectations mechanism is sensitive to this dependence of prices on policy, then inevitably price expectations will vary with changes in the policy regime. Policy cannot be made on the assumption that price expectations will not respond to any change in policy. It follows that models of the economy, if used to guide policy, must incorporate some mechanism for explaining how price expectations respond to policy changes.

The explanation that price expectations are formed rationally accords with the economist's idea of the appropriate use of information. Further, since it does suggest a mechanism which relates price expectations to policy changes, it is no surprise that economists have started to use rational expectations in models which do not have any neutrality implications. For example, consider a Keynesian model in which the government undertakes a stimulatory policy to combat unemployment. In a conventional Keynesian model an increase in government expenditure would have a sequence of impacts on aggregate demand. The first impact comes from the initial expenditure, the second arises from the incomes raised by the first round expenditure and so on. Employment would be boosted progressively to produce the increments to aggregate demand. However, if employers have rational expectations, the whole shift to the new equilibrium could take place in a single step. Employment would jump to the new level immediately. Thus the rationality of expectations enhances the potency of a stimulatory policy in a Keynesian world by shortening the adjustment process.

The original proponents of rational expectations in macroeconomics are not impressed with this application of their ideas. Typically they refuse to consider the possibility of expectations being formed rationally in the context of a model which features other behaviour which is not obviously rational. For instance, they might argue that a Keynesian model depends upon the assumption that the wage rate is fixed, that they know no model of rational behaviour which would produce a fixed wage rate, so it is silly to assume rationality of expectations within such a model. They thus place great store on the internal consistency of models. Macro models are considered '*ad hoc*' unless they are based on a consistent general equilibrium framework. But such models generally exhibit money neutrality.

In a sense the proponents of rational expectations seek to reduce macroeconomics to consistent microeconomic foundations, but economists have spent much of the last twenty years trying to develop a consistent microeconomic basis for macroeconomics with but little conspicuous success. The general equilibrium model of utility and profit maximising behaviour provides a consistent model of the behaviour of an economy based on individuals. Macroeconomics, on the other hand, is essentially concerned with aggregates, with overall demand, with *the* price level and with aggregate employment. The quantity theory of money is an aggregate notion as is the Keynesian consumption function. While many of the ideas that inspire macro concepts like the consumption function are derived from individual behaviour, macro models are necessarily highly aggregated. Nobody has yet been able to reconcile the macro and micro levels adequately. Macroeconomists continue to use models which are not based upon a general equilibrium framework and there is no evidence that they perform worse than do their equilibrium-oriented counterparts. Thus the challenge of the rational expectations theorists that other macroeconomists should forsake work based on '*ad hoc*' models has had little effect.

In summary the effect of rational expectations theorists on the practice of macroeconomics has been considerable. The proposition that one must allow for expectations to change when policy alters has been widely accepted. This has led to a reassessment of the possibilities for stabilisation policies and to a lessening in fine-tuning ambitions. However, the apprehension which rational expectations theorists have about using the rational expectations approach in '*ad hoc*' models has not been accepted. Practitioners have tended to adopt the good ideas which have been generated and to pay little attention to the prohibitions.

7.2 Have Rational Expectations Theorists Succeeded on their Own Terms?

It is quite clear that the appearance of the rational expectations research programme within macroeconomics has influenced the way macroeconomic theorising and testing is carried out. But what of its success as a new line of research in its own right? This opens up a general methodological question of just how one should evaluate economic research. The criteria we prefer to use are (i) whether the line of research has generated new theoretical ideas, and (ii) whether those new ideas have attracted substantial empirical support.

We do not propose trying to decide directly whether the rational expectations macrotheory has performed better or worse than some alternative theory. In this we differ from the simple tests of theory which are suggested in most economics text books. The usual practice indicates that theory choice is based on a simple hypothesis test. Theory A becomes the null hypothesis, theory B the alternative hypothesis and the statistical test decides, within confidence limits, which is true. But since we have seen in the previous chapters how easily statistical results can be overturned we should be extremely sceptical of such crucial experiments. Rather than relying on a single decisive experiment we are suggesting that the progress of the rational expectations programme be inferred from an evaluation of the way in which it has evolved. Has it tended to stimulate new ideas and have these new ideas found support in the data?

By these criteria, the rational expectations programme seems to have failed. While the ability to produce an increasing range of theoretical models has been demonstrated it is clear that these models have attracted little empirical support. The original proposition that macroeconomic policy would have no effect even in the short run was novel. Earlier writers in the monetarist tradition, notably Milton Friedman, had insisted that there could be no lasting trade-off between unemployment and inflation. But the early rational expectations models went much further in predicting no possibility of exploiting such a trade-off even in the short-run.

The statistical proposition that was distilled from this theoretical novelty was that the level of unemployment in the economy was given by the natural rate for that economy and could not be affected by demand management policies. This proposition was tested a number of times, mainly by Thomas Sargent. None of the experiments was very convincing and even Sargent was forced to conclude that the rational expectations predictions were merely 'not obscenely at variance with the data' (Sargent, 1976a, p.233).

It proved to be quite easy to extend the rational expectations models by enriching the demand side. More complicated models of the money market were added which allowed testing of propositions about the real and nominal interest rates. In this way the rational expectations models proved quite fruitful, although these extensions also had difficulty in attracting convincing empirical support. The ease with which rational expectations models could produce new results provides part of the reason for their rapid adoption in a variety of areas of economics. The original proponents of the rational expectations approach decried much of this as '*ad hoc*'. Clearly they were trying to impose some external criteria to test the purity of the ideas which could be associated with their research programme. They argued that unless macro models were developed from a consistent general equilibrium framework it could not be regarded as other than *ad hoc*. In practice it seems that the actual test they implied was that the work should incorporate the natural rate hypothesis.

But even the natural rate hypothesis was under some challenge. The early research of Lucas and Sargent had assumed that under the natural rate hypothesis the deviation of employment from the natural rate would be independent of all anticipated policy. The failure of the tests conducted by Sargent seems to have convinced Lucas (and presumably Sargent) that models had to be developed which allowed past variations in policy to affect current unemployment. It was clear that current unemployment was related to past policy. To reconcile this with policy impotence they needed to demonstrate that it was the *unanticipated* components of past policy levels which had a persistent effect. If correctly-anticipated past policy had a continuing influence then clearly policy was not impotent. So Lucas developed a model in which errors in the anticipation of policy were incorporated into decisions to buy capital equipment and hence influenced future production and employment levels.

This ability of the rational expectations theorists to manipulate their model to deal with an empirical failure may demonstrate the robustness of the theory. But it is probably better seen as a reflection of the ingenuity of the theorists. Faced with a specific failure of a theory one would normally expect theorists to be able to make a modification to rectify the specific failure. Our test of the programme is whether making this modification produced some new theoretical insight which attracted empirical support.

The new theoretical insight is not clear. Perhaps it is the suggestion that the aniticipated and unanticipated components of demand policy can have quite separate effects. Certainly the new empirical tests of the programme were developed on the basis of this observation. Their specific thrust was that no anticipated component of policy, present or past, could cause unemployment to deviate from its natural rate. Tests along these lines appeared to attract some support for the now-modified rational expectations programme. Barro split policy into anticipated and unanticipated components and found that the former exerted no influence on the real variables. Unfortunately for the programme, however, Mishkin (1982) subsequently produced further results which overturned Barro's. Again, rational expectations macrotheory was left without empirical support.

Two features of Mishkin's results suggest possible ways forward for rational expectations theorists. First, he found that the rational expectations assumption fared better in his tests than did that of neutrality assumption. This reinforces the movement in macroeconomics to apply the assumption that expectations are formed rationally without imposing neutrality. Clearly the results provide some justification for ignoring the strictures on 'ad hockery' voiced by Lucas, Sargent and Wallace. The other possibility opened up by Mishkin's work is to find some other specification of the neutrality proposition. It may be possible to re-define the notion of neutrality so as to overcome the empirical weaknesses revealed by Mishkin.

7.3 Conclusion

Macroeconomic theory was in a crisis in the early 1970s. Expectations of macroeconomic theory were high. A general perception had developed during the long boom that government policy based on macroeconomic theory could be used to avoid depressions and recessions. Yet industrialised economies were plagued by the simultaneous occurrence of high inflation and high unemployment. This persistent stagflation posed a severe challenge to macroeconomics. Out of this crisis a new variant of macroeconomic theory emerged. Deviations from the natural rate of unemployment were explained exclusively by errors in anticipations and expectations were argued to be formed rationally. Thus there was no basis for systematic deviation in unemployment. Superficially this variant of macrotheory was appealing. It explained how high levels of inflation and unemployment could co-exist without providing any possibility of an active policy of demand-stimulation in lessening unemployment. It tended to support the general conservative shift in world politics that was apparent at the time. Governments could do no good and plenty of harm, so it was best that they should not be too involved in the economy.

Some aspects of the theory were extremely appealing to economists. The idea that expectations were formed rationally – unbiassed and based on all available information – seemed sensible to those economists accustomed to the standard neo-classical models of economic behaviour. While this aspect of the new research programme appealed to many economists, the idea that deviations from the natural rate were based exclusively on errors in expectations seemed rather more questionable. So a variety of non-neutral models have been constructed.

Economists working in rational expectations tradition tended to ridicule these non-neutral models as '*ad hoc*'. By this they meant that the models were not usually based on general equilibrium micro-level premises but rather postulated as aggregate relationships. They argued that those who challenged the neutrality models did so on the basis of unreal assumptions. While the realism of assumptions in all economic theories may be open to question, most of us accept that models which are able to develop and substantiate empirical hypotheses are preferred to those which cannot. The rational expectations models failed because they could not attract very much empirical evidence in support of their propositions.

The first failure of testing rational expectations models led to changes in the nature of the theory. The natural rate proposition was changed to allow both *past* and *current* errors in expectations to have an effect on unemployment where the earlier version had postulated that only current errors were important. The modified form of the programme attracted some empirical support but did not remain unchallenged for long. The way forward for the believers in this research programme seems to be to limit further the specification of the neutrality proposition.

For economists and students of economics, there are a number of lessons to be learnt from the development of this research programme. First and foremost is the observation that private actors will almost certainly change their behaviour in response to a government policy. Second, the change may well be that predicted by assuming that private actions have rational expectations of government policy. Third, macroeconomic research programmes are entities which evolve and interact with one another at the level of ideas (for example, the idea that expectations are formed rationally has been adopted widely) and at the level of data (for example, the persistence challenge). An understanding of the way programmes evolve and develop may help us contribute to that process.

References

Addison, J. T. and Burton, J. (1982) 'Keynes' Analysis of Wages and Unemployment Revisited', *Manchester School*, 1–23.

Aiginger, K. (1980) 'Empirical Evidence on the Rational Expectations Hypothesis Using Reported Expectations', Paper Presented to the World Congress of Econometric Society, Aix en Provence.

Akerlof, G. A. (1979) 'The Case against Conservative Macroeconomics: An Inaugural Lecture', *Economica*, 46 (183), August, 219–37.

Barro, R. J. (1977) 'Unanticipated Money Growth and Unemployment in the United States', *American Economic Review*, 67, March, 101–15.

Barro, R. J. (1979) 'Unanticipated Money Growth and Unemployment in the United States: Reply', *American Economic Review*, 69, December, 1004–9.

Barro, R. J. and Rush, M. (1980) 'Unanticipated Money and Economic Activity' in S. Fischer (ed.) *Rational Expectations and Economic Policy* (NBER/University of Chicago Press).

Blaug, M. (1980) *The Methodology of Economics* (Cambridge University Press).

Blinder, A. S. and Fischer, S. (1981) 'Inventories, Rational Expectations and the Business Cycle', *Journal of Monetary Economics*, B, November, 277–304.

Branson, W. H. (1979) *Macroeconomic Theory and Policy*, 2nd edn (Harper & Row).

Brown, B. and Maital, S. (1981) 'What Do Economists Know? An Empirical Study of Experts' Expectations', *Econometrica*, 49, March, 491–504.

Buiter, W. H. (1980) 'The Macroeconomics of Dr Pangloss: A Critical Survey of the New Classical Macroeconomics', *Economic Journal*, 90, March, 34–50.

Cagan, P. (1956) 'The Monetary Dynamics of Hyperinflation' in M. Friedman (ed.) *Studies in the Quantity Theory of Money* (University of Chicago Press).

Cherry, R., Clawson, P. and Dean, J. W. (1981/2) 'Microfoundations of Macrorational Expectations Models', *Journal of Post Keynesian Economics*, 4, Winter, 214–30.

Clark, K. B. and Summers, L. H. (1979) 'Labour Market Dynamics and Unemployment: a Reconsideration', *Brookings Papers on Economic Activity*, 13–60.

Coase, R. H. and Fowler, R. F. (1935) 'Bacon Production and the Pig-cycle in Great Britain', *Economica*, May, 142–67.

Davidson, P. (1972) *Money and the Real World* (Macmillan/Wiley).

De Canio, S. (1979) 'Rational Expectations and Learning from Experience', *Quarterly Journal of Economics*, February, 47–57.

Feldstein, M., Green, J. and Sheshinski, E. (1978) 'Inflation and Taxes in a Growing Economy with Debt and Equity Finance', *Journal of Political Economy*, 86, April, 853–70.

Fisher, S. (1977) 'Long-term Contracts, Rational Expectations and the Optimal Money Supply Rule', *Journal of Political Economy*, 85, February, 191–206.

Fisher, I. (1926) 'A Statistical Relation between Unemployment and Price Changes', *International Labour Review*, 13, June, 185–92; reprinted in *Journal of Political Economy*, 81, March–April 1973, 496–502.

Friedman, M. (1975) *Essays in Positive Economics* (University of Chicago Press).

Friedman, M. (1968) 'The Role of Monetary Policy', *American Economic Review*, 58, March, 1–17.

Gordon, R. J. (ed.) *Milton Friedman's Monetary Framework: A Debate with his Critics* (University of Chicago Press).

Gordon, R. J. (1976) 'Recent Developments in the Theory of Inflation and Unemployment', *Journal of Monetary Economics*, 2, April, 185–220.

Gordon, R. J. (1981) 'Output Fluctuations and Gradual Price Adjustment', *Journal of Economic Literature*, 19, June, 493–530.

Gottman, J. M. (1981) *Time-Series Analysis: A Comprehensive Introduction for Social Scientists* (Cambridge University Press).

Hall, R. E. (1975) 'The Rigidity of Wages and the Persistence of Unemployment', *Brookings Papers on Economic Activity*, 2, 301–49.

Hoel, M. (1979) 'Rational Expectations and Rigid Wages: A Model of Inflation and Unemployment', *Scandinavian Journal of Economics*, 81 (3), 387–99.

Johnson, H. G. (1978a) 'A Survey of Theories of Inflation', in *Selected Essays in Monetary Economics* (George Allen & Unwin) originally published in *Indian Economic Review*, 6, August 1963.

Johnson, H. G. (1978b) 'Money in a Neo-classical One-sector Growth Model', in *Selected Essays in Monetary Economics* (George Allen & Unwin) originally published in Johnson, H. G. *Essays in Monetary Economics* (George Allen & Unwin, 1967).

Keynes, J. M. (1930) *A Treatise on Money* (Macmillan Harcourt Brace).

Keynes, J. M. (1936) *The General Theory of Employment, Interest and Money* (Macmillan).

Kuhn, T. S. (1970) *The Structure of Scientific Revolutions* 2nd edn (University of Chicago Press).

Lakatos, I. (1970) 'Falsification and the Methodology of Scientific Research Programmes', in Lakatos, I. and Musgrave A. E. (eds) *Criticism and the Growth of Knowledge* (Cambridge University Press) pp.91–196.

Leiderman, L. (1980) 'Macroeconometric Testing of the Rational Expectations and Structural Neutrality Hypotheses for the United States', *Journal of Monetary Economics*, 6(1) January, 69–82.

Lucas, R. E. (1972) 'Testing the Natural Rate Hypothesis', in Eckstein, O. (ed) *The Econometrics of Price Determination* (Federal Reserve Board, Washington) 50–9.

Lucas, R. E. (1973) 'Some International Evidence on Output-inflation Trade-off', *American Economic Review*, 63, June, 326–34.

Lucas, R. E. (1975) 'An Equilibrium Model of the Business Cycles', *Journal of Political Economy*, 83, December, 1113–44.

McCallum, B. T. (1980) 'The Significance of Rational Expectations Theory', *Challenge*, January/February, 37–43.

McNees, S. K. (1978) 'The "Rationality" of Economic Forecasts', *American Economic Review*, 68, May, 301–5.

Maddock, R. (1984) 'Rational Expectations Macrotheory: A Lakatosian Case Study in Programme Adjustment', *History of Political Economy*, forthcoming.

Maddock, R and Carter, M. G. (1982) 'A Child's Guide's to Rational Expectations', *Journal of Economic Literature*, 20, March, 39–51.

Metzler, L. (1941) 'The Nature and Stability of Inventory Cycles', *Review of Economies and Statistics*, 23, August, 113–29.

Mills, E. S. (1962) *Price, Output and Inventory Policy: A Study of the Economics of the Firm and the Industry* (Wiley).

Mishkin, F. S. (1982) 'Does Anticipated Monetary Policy Matter? An Econometric Investigation', *Journal of Political Economy*, 90, February, 22–51.

Modigliani, F. (1977) 'The Monetarist Controversy or, Should We Forsake Stabilization Policies?', *American Economic Review*, 67, March, 1–19.

Muth, J. (1961) 'Rational Expectations and the Theory of Price Movements', *Econometrica*, 29, July, 315–35.

Nelson, C. R. (1975) 'Rational Expectations and the Predictive Efficiency of Economic Models', *Journal of Business*, 48, 331–343.

Okun, A. M. (1981) *Prices and Quantities: A Macroeconomic Analysis* (Brookings).

Pearce, D. (1979) 'Comparing Survey and Rational Measures of Expected Inflation. Forecast Performance and Interest Rate Effects', *Journal of Money, Credit and Banking*, 11, November, 447–56.

Phelps, E. S. and Taylor, J. B. (1977) 'Stabilizing Powers of Monetary Policy under Rational Expectations', *Journal of Political Economy*, 85, February, 163–90.

Phillips, A. W. (1958) 'The Relation Between Unemployment and the Rate of Change of Money Wage Rates in the United Kingdom, 1861–1957', *Economica*, 25, November, 283–99.

Popper, K. R. (1959) *The Logic of Scientific Discovery* (Hutchinson).

Popper, K. R. (1962) *Conjectures and Refutations* (Basic Books).

Priestley, M. B. (1981) *Spectral Analysis and Time Series* (Academic Press).

Sargent, T.J. (1973) 'Rational Expectations, the Real Rate of Interest and the Natural Rate of Unemployment', *Brookings Papers on Economic Activity*, 2, 429–72.

Sargent, T. J. (1976a) 'A Classical Macroeconomic Model for the United States', *Journal of Political Economy*, 84, April, 207–37.

Sargent, T. J. (1976b) 'Testing for Neutrality and Rationality', in *A Prescription for Monetary Policy: Proceedings from a Seminar Series* (Federal Reserve Bank of Minneapolis).

Sargent, T. J. and Wallace, N. (1975) 'Rational' Expectations, the Optimal Monetary Instrument and the Optimal Money Supply Rule', *Journal of Political Economy*, 83, 241–55.

Shiller, R. J. (1978) 'Rational Expectations and the Dynamic Structure of Macroeconomic Models: A Critical Review', *Journal of Monetary Economics*, 4, January, 1–44.

Small, D. H. (1979) 'Unanticipated Money Growth and Unemployment in the United States: Comment', *American Economic Review*, 69, December, 996–1003.

Taylor, J. B. (1975) 'Monetary Policy During a Transition to Rational Expectations', *Journal of Political Economy*, 83, October, 1009–21.

Tobin, J. (1965) 'Money and Economic Growth', *Econometrica*, 33, October, 671–84.

Trevithick, J. A. (1980) *Inflation: A Guide to the Crisis in Economics*, 2nd edn (Penguin).

Turnovsky, S. (1970) 'Empirical Evidence on the Formation of Price Expectations', *Journal of the American Statistical Association*, 65, December, 1441–54.

Wallis, K. F. (1980) 'Econometric Implications of the Rational Expectations Hypothesis', *Econometrica*, 48 (1), January, 49–73.

Wold, H. (1938) *A Study in the Analysis of Time Series* (Uppsala: Almqvist & Wiksell).

Author Index

162

Subject Index